HE GA
JESUS IN

ENDORSEMENT

My friend Luke Walker has written a wonderful book for pastors and the people they lead, as well as for unbelievers. The subtitle, *Jesus in the Book of Judges*, tips readers as to the direction of the discussion. Walker finds aspects of our Lord's person and work prefigured in the persons and actions of the Judges, and I think he is right to do so. One of the many treats of this book is the vignettes into the hermeneutical method utilized throughout. Viewing the Old Testament as God preparing the world for the incarnation, sufferings, and glory of the Son of God, this book helps readers understand not only *that* God prepared the world for Christ but *how*. Historical figures and their acts often point beyond them to a much greater figure and his much greater acts. The historical figures and some of their acts pointing to the future find their terminus or target in our Lord Jesus Christ. Christ is the bull's eye of Holy Scripture, everything in it pointing to Him (the OT) or explaining the fact that He has come (the NT). The end of the biblical narrative is much better than its beginning and middle, but the end is hinted at all along the way in persons, places, institutions, and events. I highly recommend *He Gave Them Judges*.

Richard C. Barcellos, Ph.D.
Grace Reformed Baptist Church, Palmdale, CA
Author of *Better than the Beginning: Creation in Biblical Perspective*

HE GAVE THEM JUDGES

JESUS IN THE BOOK OF JUDGES

LUKE WALKER

After that he gave them judges…
Acts 13:20

WRATH AND GRACE PUBLISHING

Dedicated to
My friend Johan Henao,
And the saints of Redeeming Cross,
Past, present, and future.

TABLE OF CONTENTS

PREFACE

Reformed and Calvinistic theologians of our day have made significant advances with regard to *redemptive-historical* and *biblical-theological* elements of hermeneutics. For far too long, the church has lacked clear and concise resources explaining—in a focused way—*redemptive-historical* principles from the Scriptures themselves as well as models by which the student of Scripture may deductively glean these principles. Over the past century and a half, Reformed theologians have finally begun to give these branches of theology—long *integrated* into the writings of theologians in nearly every epoch of the Christian Church—a due consideration. Building on the contributions of many of the 16th Century Reformers, 17th Century English Puritans, theologians of the Dutch Second Reformation (*Nadre Reformatie*), 19th Century Scottish Presbyterians and 19th Century English Baptists (*e.g.* Charles Spurgeon), theologians such as Geerhardus Vos, Herman Ridderbos, Edmund Clowney, Richard Gaffin and Sinclair Ferguson have helped spearhead a resurgence of interest in Christological hermeneutics in the 20th and 21st Centuries (*e.g.* see the principles set out in Sinclair Ferguson's 2002 Proclamation Truth pamphlet, "Preaching Christ from the Old Testament"). As a result of these men's labors, preaching in the Reformed and Calvinistic churches has become more consistently "Christ-centered" and *redemptive-historical* in nature. For many, this is viewed as a welcomed development. For others, it is viewed with a great deal of reservation.

While the *redemptive-historical* element has begun to come to its own in hermeneutics, there are still many debates about how to apply the principles of redemptive history to biblical interpretation—especially with regard to our interpretation of the Old Testament Scriptures. An excessive and unsubstantiated fear of falling into what some believe to be an illegitimate and allegorical method of interpretation has hindered quite a number within the Reformed camp from fully embracing a *redemptive-historical* approach to a text. Fanciful attempts to see Jesus in all the Scriptures have sometimes amounted to "seeing Jesus where he isn't," and, as a result, have only further served to hinder the consistent appropriation of the *redemptive-historical* element of biblical interpretation. The imbalance, felt on both sides, leaves many onlookers either disinterested or disillusioned with the entire enterprise. What can be done?

In recent years, certain publishers have turned the sermons of Reformed preachers into homiletical commentaries. In this way, sermons have become hermeneutical guides for seminarians, pastors and theologians. This is a welcomed development insofar as such commentaries serve to integrate a more full-orbed hermeneutical approach into our homiletics. Iain Duguid's works on *Abraham, Isaac and Jacob, Numbers, Esther & Ruth, Song of Songs* and *Daniel* are among the most helpful examples when it comes to integrating the *biblical-theological* element of the interpretive aspect into the preaching of the Old Testament. However, a great need remains for the publication of more works of this nature on Old Testament books. Enter Luke Walker's work on Judges.

Judges is one of the richest of the Old Testament narratival books—yet one of the most overlooked by commentators. Some of this neglect exists, no doubt, on account of the place that the book holds in redemptive history. Judges forms "the no-man's-land" between the Exodus, wilderness wandering, conquest of Canaan and the establishment of the Kingdom. It is far easier to connect the Exodus motif to Christ, since the Evangelists and the Apostles do that explicitly for us (*e.g.* Luke 9:31; John 19:36 and 1 Cor. 5:7). Additionally, the New Testament is replete with references to the connection between the Covenant promises concerning the Kingdom and the Christ. However, the New Testament is virtually silent about the period of the Judges (except for one reference in Heb. 11).

One might rightly think of the Judges as precursors of the Kings of Israel. When viewed that way, one can easily make the connection between the Judges and the Savior. In a very real sense, Jesus is the Judge of Judges. All of the Judges serve to highlight some aspect of the redeeming work of God. Whether it is the unlikely nature of the judge himself or the unexpected way in which the judge gains the victory over the kingdom of darkness, the multiplicity of judges are preparing the minds and hearts of the people for a true and greater judge. In this book, Luke Walker features cameos of seven of the judges in the book. He considers the judges in both their *historical* and *redemptive-*

historical contexts. Writing with a devotional aim, Walker draws our attention to the way in which each judge highlights and foreshadows some aspect of the Person and work of Christ. As we come to understand these foreshadowings, we better come to understand why "He gave them judges."

Nick Batzig
New Covenant Presbyterian Church
Richmond Hill, GA

ACKNOWLEDGMENTS

I am deeply indebted to the work of wiser and godlier men than I. John Owen, Charles Spurgeon, Geerhardus Vos, Edmund Clowney, Art Azurdia, Sinclair Ferguson, Richard Barcellos, Nick Batzig, and many more, have all paved the way for me in these matters. I have simply applied their work to the book of Judges.

I would like to express my deepest gratitude to God for my beautiful wife Angel and her countless hours of help on this and all my projects. Thank you to my editing team: Brady Erickson, Nick Larson, Zach "Sneaky Z" Larson, Daniel Stanley, Franky Collazo, and Carlos Gonzalez; to Johan Henao for his great support and encouragement; to Paul Hidgon for his wise counsel; to Richard Barcellos and Nick Batzig for reading the work and adding their generous words to it; and to my co-elder Gottfried Caspari and my church family at Redeeming Cross, thank you for your support and prayers. You are all priceless blessings to me.

I would not have even made the attempt at this book without the hearty encouragements of my dear friend David Torres. Thank you brother.

May the Triune God procure glory for himself from this small offering.

INTRODUCTION

It is perhaps needful to set some things in place before we begin. The pages of this book are littered with hermeneutical tangents relevant to the material at hand; yet laying some basic groundwork up front is not out of order.

I preached and wrote this book under the happy persuasion that every passage of Scripture points to our Lord Jesus Christ in one way or another. I realize that by such a sweeping statement I have put myself in *critical* danger of a wrist slapping, but I care not. If I am in error, it is a safer error than the modern one, which is nothing short of a Christless exposition of Scripture. We live in a day of Christless preaching; the lambs need more of him than ever. What Richard Sibbes said of another matter, I say in my own defense here: "I had rather hazard the censure of some, than hinder the good of others."[1]

But I do not believe myself to be in error. Christ's own assertions are unintelligible to me if I take them to mean anything less than what we here propose (Luke 24:26-27, 44-47; John 5:39). And besides, the greatest expositors and preachers in church history are squarely on my side.[2] Unless we search out Christ in the entirety of Scripture, we are cheating ourselves and will come off our reading of it

---

[1] Richard Sibbes, *The Works of Richard Sibbes* (Edingburgh: Banner of Truth Trust, 2001), 1:41.

[2] Time would fail to speak of Chrysostom, Owen, Edwards, and Spurgeon. See Christopher A. Hall, *Reading Scripture with the Church Fathers* (Downers Grove: InterVarsity Press, 1998); Richard C. Barcellos, *The Family Tree of Reformed Biblical Theology* (Owensboro: Reformed Baptist Academic Press, 2010); Joel R. Beeke and Mark Jones, *A Puritan Theology: Doctrine for Life* (Grand Rapids: Reformation Heritage Books, 2012), 706-07.

just as confused and dejected as the two disciples were on the road to Emmaus. It's my chief desire in writing that you would join me in this blessed persuasion.

God's redemptive works in history and the people he used to work them are all anticipatory of the coming promised Seed of the woman (Gen. 3:15). This first promise of the gospel, known as the *protoevangelium,* echoes throughout the Old Testament in what God did and who he used to do it; these works of God are called *types and shadows.* They are copies of Jesus Christ. He is the great shadow caster; all his types are moving miniatures of himself. They were designed to help the people recognize him ahead of time, as well as to display him to us now. Biblical history is patterned after the coming eschatological man, and the judges are no exception. Thus, we will expect to find them mimicking Christ, as shadow imitates substance.

If there's any doubt that this applies specifically to the book of Judges, let us go, as commanded, *to the law and to the testimony!* Consider the words of Isaiah. He said another Judge was to come: "When they cry to the LORD because of oppressors, he will send them a savior and defender, and deliver them" (Isa. 19:20). When Isaiah spoke of a last days deliverance that would include not only Israel but Egypt and Assyria as well, he used *judges* language to describe the One who would do it. Yes, according to the testimony of Isaiah the prophet, Jesus is the great, final, global Judge to come.

In the present work, we will look at the lives and times of seven of the judges, utilizing a redemptive-historical hermeneutic to unearth how God stunningly foreshadowed the person and work of his Son in these remarkable figures. May our hearts burn within us while he opens to us the Scriptures!

Luke Walker
May 2017
Richfield, MN

CONCERNING JUDGES

Who were the judges? Ruth 1:1 says, "In the days when the judges ruled" or "governed." The judges were rulers of Israel for a brief space in history, forerunners to the kings who would rise later. They had no succession but were raised up here and there as the Lord saw fit. The people who didn't experience the wonders of God in the generations of Moses had forgotten his great deeds of deliverance. They failed to destroy all the peoples of the land as the Lord had commanded them and, just as he had spoken, the peoples became a snare to them. They fell away and worshiped the Baals and the Asheroth and the gods of the nations, about which God had warned them. God in his justice handed the people over to oppressors, so that they served under the iron fists of wicked kings. But in time they groaned in their slavery, called upon the Lord, and he gave them judges.

CHAPTER 1
GETTING THERE

After the death of Joshua…

Judges 1:1

We are to spend our study in ancient Israel. To help us feel the antiquity of the times, let's travel there together across the expanses of the past. Allow me to picture human history as a city so as to make our journey more vivid.

As we walk out the front door of this century, we find ourselves on the cutting edge of the developing future. Stepping onto the sidewalk and turning left, we notice that our two next-door neighbors are the great English preachers Martyn Lloyd-Jones and Charles Spurgeon. The mailboxes on our street bear such esteemed names as J. Owen, J. Calvin, and M. Luther, and the last and oldest house on the block belongs to one Master John Wycliffe, who lives at 1320 Protestant Way. At the end of the block, we jump on a light rail to make our journey more swiftly.

Several blocks down the road we see hospice vehicles in front of an old British man's house, and through the window we catch him laboring out words to a young scribe. It's old Bede, finishing his translation of John with his dying breath. A few blocks more and we spy a North African man writing at a table on his front porch. We can just barely make out the title of the book in which he writes: *Confessions*. It's Augustine!

A few more blocks and we reach the city square, where we find apostles preaching on every corner. In the center of town stands a bloody cross, and a mighty One is walking in the midst of the people. As we pass the square and make our way to the other side of town, we meet the prophet Malachi pointing back emphatically toward the center of the city and saying something about a coming Messenger. Over the next several blocks prophets are standing on every corner, all of them pointing in the same direction and thundering out the glories of the Lord. Isaiah and Jeremiah, Ezekiel with his locks, and Jonah in clothes still dripping with salt water.

Next, we encounter a caravan of white SUVs, and I think I smell coffee coming from the windows. As we pass, we glance back and notice the license plate of the lead vehicle reads SHEBA. They're headed for a kingly mansion with seven steps leading to a magnificent front door, hewn of immaculate cedar. It's the palace of King Solomon.

As we continue our journey, the city begins to spread out. We pass over battlefields where David and his mighty men are doing glorious deeds in the power of God. As much as we'd like to stop and watch them, we must keep moving. After a short time, our train begins to slow. We pass a house where a sweet looking woman is sewing a little robe for her son. Presently we come to a stop, exit the train, and our feet touch the land of Israel.

This ground contains the bones of Joseph. In fact, Joshua has just joined him. As we walk through the land we overhear a kinsman redeemer boasting about his new wife in the city gates. We travel the length and breadth of the land and find the people in disarray. One thing we do not find is a crown. Our Guide turns around and says, "There's no king of Israel in these days, and everyone does what's right in his own eyes. Welcome to the age of the judges."

CHAPTER 2
OTHNIEL

But when the people of Israel cried out to the LORD, the LORD raised up a deliverer for the people of Israel, who saved them, Othniel the son of Kenaz.

Judges 3:9

Othniel spearheads the line of judges. Chapter 1 tells us that he was Caleb's nephew. You may remember what God had said about his uncle Caleb: "But my servant Caleb, because he has a different spirit and has followed me fully, I will bring into the land into which he went, and his descendants shall possess it" (Num. 14:24). When the people began to take the land, Caleb reminded Joshua of God's promise and went up single-handedly (at the sprightly age of 85) to take the city of Hebron. Othniel appears in the verses that follow:

From there they went against the inhabitants of Debir. The name of Debir was formerly Kiriath-sepher. And Caleb said, "He who attacks Kiriath-sepher and captures it, I will give him Achsah my daughter for a wife." And Othniel the son of Kenaz, Caleb's younger brother, captured it. And he gave him Achsah his daughter for a wife (1:11-13).

This tells us that Othniel was battle-tested at the time of his calling. He had already captured the castle and won the fair damsel. Thus, God chose a proven man who shared in the spirit of Caleb to be the first judge; no doubt his former conquests were preparation for this, his greater work.

Meanwhile, the people did what was evil in God's sight (3:7). They worshiped false gods, and he handed them over to the king of Mesopotamia, Cushan-rishathaim, to become his slaves. After eight years, they groaned and called out to the Lord, at which time he raised up Othniel to deliver them.

Othniel hits the keynote for this ancient book by embodying the essence of a judge. Three characteristics present themselves to us in him. First, *the Spirit was upon him.* The Book of Acts is shorthand for its uninspired title, *The Acts of the Apostles.* But if we were to call that inspired account for what it really is, the title would read something like *The Acts of the Holy Spirit.* It was he who animated the early church. If any Old Testament book displays the work of the Spirit in like manner, it's the book of Judges. The Spirit of God descended upon the judges and worked mighty deeds of deliverance. It was God who saved through this elite class of warriors.

Second, *he rode out to war.* The judges were God's weapons, and as they ran their course they took up weapons of their own. They clutched swords and shields; they bent bows and hurled javelins; they swung slings, and took up even stranger weapons yet (as we will see). In the period of the judges, God's temporal deliverance of the people came through earthly warfare and the violent overthrow of their enemies. He taught the people war through the judges (3:2).

Third, once God overthrew the king of Mesopotamia, *the land had rest.* The people enjoyed an achieved peace, a form of Sabbath rest, through the work of their judges.

FURTHER UP AND FURTHER IN

If we leave the text here, we might have a fine Sunday School lesson, but we have nothing of Christ. Why does this matter? It matters because the object of the Christian's faith is Jesus Christ and him crucified (Gal. 2:20). If the Old Testament Scriptures are meant to lead us to him (and they are, John 5:39; 2 Tim. 3:15), then the passage before us is no exception. With this in mind, the question is not, "Does Judges chapter 3 point to Jesus?" The question is, "*How* does Judges chapter 3 point to Jesus?" We'll spend the rest of this chapter seeking out our answer.

What is the summary of this passage? "When the people of Israel cried out to the LORD, the LORD raised up a deliverer for the people of Israel, who saved them" (3:9). In other words, God is a saving God, and he can save his people through a human savior. Shall we take another pass over the text? This time, we'll look at things from a slightly different angle—a more biblically informed angle. We will draw a bit closer and square up with the life and times of Othniel as I retell the tale.

God handed his people over to a ruthless ruler of the ancient world for their sin. We don't know much about him. He was the king of Mesopotamia, and you don't become that without an iron fist. Beyond that, we know his name, which signifies *double evil*. Let's call him the evil one. In righteous judgment, God handed his sinning people over to the evil one, to be held captive by him to do his will. But the people grew intolerant of their slavery, cried out to God, and he "raised up a deliverer for the people of Israel who saved them" (3:9).

The deliverer, as we know, is Othniel; he was a lion of a man. In fact, his name means *lion of God*. And, if you're paying attention, you already know what tribe he's from: Judah (he was the nephew of the Judean warrior Caleb). Thus we assert that Judges chapter 3 is about a lion from the tribe of Judah who saves his people by overthrowing the evil one who held them captive because of their sin. Might God be saying something here? Yes, *the eschatological Lion of Judah was coming.*

He was to have the Spirit without measure in a mightier way than any who went before him. Through the power of the Spirit, he would overthrow the enemies of God and free his people. Our Lord Jesus is the true Spirit-empowered Savior: "The Spirit of the Lord is upon me, because he has anointed me…to proclaim liberty to the captives" (Luke 4:18).

Further up and further in! Othniel didn't ride out to throw hands in an alley fight or rumble in a neighborhood skirmish; he rode out to *war*, a war to end the matter. He was a finisher, and the same is true of Christ. He is tender in mercy, but he is terrible in might. He put away sin and said, "It is finished." He is decisive. The wicked flee seven ways before him when the Lamb of God rides out to war.

"The LORD gave Cushan-rishathaim king of Mesopotamia into his hand. And his hand prevailed over Cushan-rishathaim" (3:10). The potentate was overpowering God's people, and they were powerless to free themselves from his grip. But God raised up one from among them, clothed him with power from on high, and made him stronger than the tyrant.

Consider another passage:

> Of old you spoke in a vision to your godly one, and said: 'I have granted help to one who is mighty; I have exalted one chosen from the people. I have found David, my servant; with my holy oil I have anointed him, so that my hand shall be established with him; my arm also shall strengthen him. The enemy shall not outwit him; the wicked shall not humble him. I will crush his foes before him and strike down those who hate him (Psa. 89:19-23).

Here we have notes of a mightier one than Othniel whose hand was strengthened by God against the oppressor, further foreshadows of the coming Son. It was Jesus himself who said, "When a strong man, fully armed, guards his own palace, his goods are safe; but when one stronger than he attacks him, he takes away his armor in which he trusted and divides his spoil" (Luke 11:21-22). Jesus Christ is the *stronger than he* who stripped the devil of his armor and plundered us from his legions. He overcame them, being stronger than their king. With power in his hand, he smashes doors of bronze and preaches peace to spiritual prisoners. He is the true Strong One.

When this remarkable warrior named Othniel arose, there may have been anticipation among the people of Israel who remembered God's ancient promise in the *protoevangelium*. Perhaps those who believed were thinking, "Is this he who will deal that decisive blow to the serpent?" For them it was not yet; it was their lot to greet that promise from afar, to salute him who was to come. But for us, he has come. We look up to the One who has crushed the head of the serpent with a wounded heal. He is the true Seed.

After Othniel prevailed, the land had rest. He won a time of peace and rest for the people, in anticipation of the final Rest to come. They rested from war, but not only that: their hearts were turned back to God. "So the land had rest for forty years. Then Othniel the son of Kenaz died. And the people of Israel again did what was evil in the sight of the LORD" (3:11-12). This deliverance was strong, but temporary. In record time, the majority forsook God. "Whenever the judge died, they turned back and were more corrupt than their fathers, going after other gods, serving them and bowing down to them" (2:19).

Their freedom was bound up with the life of the judge.

As long as he lived, they enjoyed it. Othniel was a passing shadow; Jesus is the true Judge who *ever* lives, and throughout all the days of his life God delivers his people. To borrow an expression, Jesus judges by the power of an indestructible life. Glory to God, we have a judge who has already passed through death, who reigns forever, never to die again. Therefore, we live.

Illuminated by subsequent revelation, verse 11 casts a shadow of the good things to come: *So the land had rest forever, and Jesus the Son of God lives.* Cushan-rishathaim was real; the slavery was real; Othniel was real; the war was real; the blood was real; the rest was real. But you and I were born in bondage to a more wicked ruler than the king of Mesopotamia. If you're a believer, there came a time when God pricked your heart, and by his amazing grace you became intolerant of your slavery to sin and to Satan. The moment you cried for mercy, Jesus rode forth with a rod of iron and broke the devil's power, setting you free.

My friend, if you are still under the power of your sin, you need to know that the Judge of all the earth is in dead earnest. Your cosmic crimes against him deserve eternal death in hell. But you also need to know that there's a way of escape. Jesus Christ stands near and is even now calling you to himself. He is ready to set you free: "Everyone who commits sin is a slave to sin...[but] if the Son sets you free, you will be free indeed" (John 8:34, 36).

CHAPTER 3
EHUD

And Ehud came to him as he was sitting alone in his cool roof chamber. And Ehud said, "I have a message from God for you." And he arose from his seat. And Ehud reached with his left hand, took the sword from his right thigh, and thrust it into his belly.

Judges 3:20-21

The psalmist captured the book of Judges in one sentence: "Many times he delivered them" (Psa. 106:43). The Levites in Nehemiah's time added to it: "Many times you delivered them according to your mercies" (Neh. 9:28). This era saw God's manifold deliverance as he took up many deliverers, or saviors. "You gave them saviors who saved them" (Neh. 9:27).

There is only one eternal Savior, the Lord Jesus Christ, but there are many *small s* saviors who foreshadow him. John, the New Testament seer, saw many crowns on Christ's head, signifying his dominion; we might say, such is his eternal substance, that when he stands in the light of revelation he casts many shadows. And each one of these Old Testament types and shadows shows us something unique about the shape of the coming Substantial One.

We come now to the second judge, Ehud, and we believe he has something unique to tell us about the work of Christ, something that Othniel didn't tell us. Verses 12-

30 record the incident, but we will give our attention to verses 20 and 21. There we find the most striking aspects of Ehud's saving work.

A MESSAGE

Ehud had a message for Eglon, and it was a *message* indeed: "Eglon, I have a message for you," as he proceeds to sink a sword into his belly. Preach the gospel at all times, if necessary use swords. Eglon was not expecting a message of *this* sort, but neither did the Unman in Perelandra expect the thunder fists of Ransom Pendragon. Yet, after all, "What message from God but a message of vengeance can a proud rebel expect?"[3]

It was an irrefutable message. We would be justified in saying that Eglon *felt* it. A message like this comes without dispute. There was no question and answer session with the Lord and Ehud after this conversation. It was *conversation over, message delivered.* Ehud left Eglon fully persuaded of its veracity. "Let no one disregard you," was God's charge to this ancient Titus.

It was also a divine message. "I have a message *from God* for you." It wasn't Ehud's message; it was God's message to the wicked ruler. It came from the throne of the God in whose hand was Eglon's breath, and thus, with full authority and power. Eglon was no doubt "astonished

---

[3] Matthew Henry, Matthew Henry's Commentary (Condensed), Accordance electronic ed. (Altamonte Springs: OakTree Software, 1996), paragraph 1136.

at his teaching, for his message [4] possessed authority" (Luke 4:32).

It was a custom message. "I have a message from God *for you*." This *message* was custom-made for Eglon. Ehud made for himself a two-edged sword, a cubit in length (3:16). He had the fat king in mind when he measured it and said, *That'll fit.* Look closely and you can see Eglon's name etched on the steel.

God often sends messages to the wicked. He takes up his word in warnings and judgments; he even reasons and pleads with the fallen sons of Adam. God's mouth is open to the wicked and the only word coming out is "repent!" The wicked should ever fear when God says he would like a word with them.

Now, Eglon might've known this was coming. Did he ever take the time to open the sacred scrolls of his captured people? He would not have read very far before he discovered that God preached his first sermon to a wicked ruler. Yes, the first time that most marvelous of messages, *the gospel,* was uttered to creatures, Satan was in the front pew. Is it any wonder that he hates it and seeks to keep men blind to it?

This message of destruction to Eglon was a message of freedom to the oppressed people of Israel. It was aimed at their oppressor, which is to say, their freedom was its goal. In Genesis 3:15, God's threat to the devil was meant to bring his ancient people great hope. How wonderfully the

---

[4] My own rendering. The Greek is here λόγος.

Mastermind works all things together. Two birds with one stone, if you like. Christ is the Stone of offense that hits every target in one throw.

After slaying the wicked ruler, Ehud went straight to the people, blasting a trumpet and declaring liberty to the captives. He said, "Follow me! Let's rid ourselves of them." And not a single man escaped their hand. The results were as stunning as the message.

I hardly need to press the point, but Christ was also sent to assassinate our arch-oppressor with a message, *the message of the cross*. "For this reason the Son of God appeared, to destroy the works of the devil" (1 John 3:8). God first preached this message to him, and Christ drove it home at his coming. The gospel is *the* powerful, lethal, irrefutable, custom, saving message from God; Ehud's is like it.

A LEFT-HANDED MESSAGE

Ehud is introduced to us as a left-handed man. We have his name, his lineage, his tribe, and his strong hand (3:15). What does this tell us? First, that Ehud's sword went undetected into the king's presence. Eglon's guards were no doubt in the habit of patting down or at least eyeing up all visitors to the king; most men were right-handed, which means they carried their sword on their left. But this was the Lord's plan, and the sword with Eglon's name on it was brought into his presence *on the sneak*. Ehud conceal carried into the king's chamber: "he bound it on his right thigh under his clothes" (3:16).

Ehud's left-handed message was unlooked-for. He took them by surprise. He came to pay tribute, as a sign of submission, and Eglon probably expected the message from God to be a sort of exclamation point to the tribute, a further affirmation of his rule over Israel. Ehud says, "Oh yeah, I almost forgot. God wants to tell you something." "Well now," thinks the fat king, "I had better stand up for this." Behold, how off guard he is! How utterly exposed to the blade! Here he stands, alone before his assassin (and probably out of breath). God knows how to checkmate the wicked.

The devil should've been on the lookout for a left-handed attack. God did it before, and what he's done before he tends to do again, on eschatological scales. He should've known the eternal promised Deliverer was going to strike him from an unexpected place. The Son was coming to crack skulls from the left (a *south paw*, as boxing has it). Sure enough, when he appeared, his message was totally unlooked-for. Jesus is the greater Ehud, who worked eternal salvation *by surprise*. Ehud foreshadows the Seed of the Woman's unexpected strike.

In this way, the cross was perfectly tactical. Jesus feigned defeat, only to snatch the prize, Satan's head on a platter. He is the wise man who played the fool to best his unsuspecting enemies. They crucified the Lord of glory, and in so doing, glorified him. The cross even took the disciples by surprise (Luke 24:41). Satan would never have worked in Judas had he known what was in play. The fallen angel of light was in deep darkness.

Satan thought he was being paid tribute. At times, we can attribute too much to the devil, but it is also possible to attribute too little to him. For example, Scripture says he has the power of death (Heb. 2:14). He is also called, "the god of this world" (2 Cor. 4:4) and "the prince of the power of the air" (Eph. 2:2). "The whole world lies in the power of the evil one" (1 John 5:19). He has the power of death, and as the promised Savior dies, he says, "Let me get my tribute of death." But as Satan begins to celebrate at the dying gasps of Jesus of Nazareth, he hears a human voice in his ear: "I have a message from God for you: *It is finished.*" God *crossed* the serpent and broke his ankles (removed his legs entirely, in fact, Gen. 3:14).

Ehud got Eglon where it counts. Now the text doesn't say this, but I think it's safe to say that Eglon was proud of his big belly. "Eglon was a very fat man" (3:17), and he probably carried it around as a sign of his wealth and power. When Ehud crafted a sword for Eglon, under the Spirit's direction, his belly was the clear bullseye.

Now, the evil one isn't proud of his belly, but he is proud of his head, and God purposed the gospel against him in much the same way. We war against "the schemes of the devil" (Eph. 6:11). His strength is in his intelligence and subtlety. God's message for the crafty one is, "He will crush your *head,*" where it counts. In the gospel, God hatched plots from all eternity and put Satan to open shame in time and space. That ancient serpent, cunning as ever, played himself into the very center of God's will against him.

With wisdom from above, Ehud lodged the sword in Eglon's belly, but the eschatological Judge struck the ancient serpent in a more remarkable way than this. He defeated him *through death*. On the cross, God plucked Satan's sword and used it to strike off his head. Jesus pinned Satan down, threw the sword to his Father, and said: "Do it!" In piercing the Son, the Father crushed the serpent and destroyed his works, "triumphing over them in him" (Col. 2:15).

In the end, Eglon was put to open shame. His servants found him lying in a pile of his own guts and excrement; the king who ruled in pride and power breathed his last in a pool of filth. There was no honorable end for Eglon when God's judge fatally humbled him. Thousands of years later we are still looking at the open-casket dishonor of his death. Jesus put the devil to open shame like this. He split his cranium wide open with the cross, spilling his many schemes all over the floor of the cosmos. It would appear that Satan has a thing for *trees,* but he should've kept himself well clear of this one.

The people's deliverance from their arch-enemy was wrapped up in Ehud's single sword thrust. We don't know how long Othniel waged war, but Ehud did it in a moment; likewise, in one blow Jesus Christ worked our eternal salvation. Ehud's first round knockout anticipates the good things to come when God's Champ would appear.

The land enjoyed rest for 80 years, which also tells us something about the coming deliverance. Consider the time comparison: a split-second strike worked a lifetime of peace for them. Our Judge put away sin forever by the once-for-all sacrifice of himself. The Holy Spirit regenerated you in the twinkling of an eye; as he sent the message of the cross home to you he nailed you and your sins with Christ, and from that moment forward you enjoy spiritual rest for eternity. Within 80 years the believers of my generation will be resting in the paradise of God; in 80 billion years we will just be getting acclimated to our great Rest.

After triumphing over Eglon, Ehud went and summoned the people. There was more fighting to be done, but it was fighting that flowed out of the decisive victory. "Follow me," says Ehud, "for the LORD has given your enemies the Moabites into your hand" (3:28). And give them he did, for "not a man escaped" (3:29). The same can be said of our indwelling sin. From the moment of your conversion, you entered into a war with it, but God has promised you the victory, sin by sin, because of the finished work of the eschatological Ehud.

The call of Ehud is the call of Christ to all: "Follow me." He walks church aisles and city streets, wherever his triumph is preached, and calls lost sinners to himself. Even upon these very pages his voice is calling the lost children of Adam to safety. My dear reader, are you sharing in his victory?

CHAPTER 4
SHAMGAR

After him was Shamgar the son of Anath, who killed 600 of the Philistines with an oxgoad, and he also saved Israel.

Judges 3:31

Shamgar is the third judge. It would've been easy to skip over him, because he only gets one verse. But this one verse is here for good reason. God is not in the habit of wasting words; an idle word has never left his mouth! This becomes even clearer when we consider what Scripture is: God's own testimony to his Son. The Bible, cover-to-cover, is the God-breathed account of his plan to save sinners through his Son Jesus Christ. Nothing less than God's glory is at stake in Scripture; therefore, we know that even this little verse is pregnant with meaning.

What we are asserting is that every passage of Scripture finds its true meaning in the Lord Jesus Christ. The Bible is like a photo mosaic: each passage is a snapshot of Christ, and put together they form a majestic portrait of this gigantic figure. The Bible bears witness to him in the details, and in the drama; Christ crucified is the forest, and he is the trees. We heartily *amen* the words of Thomas Adams: "Christ is the sum of the whole Bible, prophesied, typified, prefigured, exhibited, demonstrated, to be found in every leaf, almost in every line, the Scriptures being but as it were the swaddling bands of the child Jesus."[5]

Now for Judges 3:31. It is undoubtedly one of the most undusted corners of Scripture; after all, when was the last time you heard a sermon on Shamgar? When we come to Shamgar—and, hearken to me here, my friends—we are *not* approaching him as an analogy. He doesn't merely make us think about Christ. He *does,* but so does every hero of old, in their own way. Scripture is something greater: The Holy Spirit's *intention* in this verse is to tell us about Jesus. He is, in fact, the Authorial intent of any given passage.

How do we get there? Like this: The Old Testament is full of events and institutions, things that God did and things he put in place, and every one of them displays or symbolizes truth to us. They show us something about God and what he's doing. Take, for example, the priesthood. What truth does the priesthood represent? Mediation through atonement. Judges 3:31 is an event, an act of God. What truth does Shamgar display? Broadly, he displays *salvation.* The brief account of Shamgar communicates to us that God is a saving God.

God's attributes and works sing at their highest pitch in Jesus Christ and him crucified. Once we have our truth in hand, we have only to ask the question, "How does this find its fulfillment in Christ?" Here in Judges 3:31, God is presented as a merciful, delivering God who sends a human champion to save. And salvation through Shamgar

---

[5] Quoted in J.I. Packer, *A Quest for Godliness: The Puritan Vision of the Christian Life* (Wheaton: Crossway, 1993), 103.

is a mere shadow of eternal salvation through Jesus Christ. So that's how we get from A to Z, from shadow to substance, from Shamgar to Jesus Christ.

SHAMGAR WAS A JUDGE

The first two words of verse 31 tell us so. "After him"—after who? After Ehud, who was after Othniel. Shamgar falls in the line of judges. So, everything we know about the work of a judge applies to Shamgar as well. That is to say, he was a raised-up, empowered, warring savior. In fact, at this time all of God's saving power was concentrated in Shamgar. There was a time when *this* is what God was doing. That's why it was written down, and that's why it's worthy of our highest consideration. "For whatever was written in former days was written for our instruction" (Rom. 15:4).

HE WAS VICTORIOUS

Othniel rode out with troops, and Ehud entered into single combat with Eglon, but here Shamgar steps onto the battlefield alone against 600 Philistines. Legendary! We throw big numbers around like we know what they are, but, I wonder if you stopped reading and began counting to 600, would you finish? 600 is *a lot*. Shamgar wasn't counting, he was killing; it was a superhuman feat of power. This one man was worth more than all their strength put together and he proved it by single-handedly decimating them all. Thus, Shamgar is the *one* who fought for the salvation of *many;* we have our truth in hand.

This truth reaches its highest and final expression as follows: "The Son of Man came...to give his life as a ransom for many" (Matt. 20:28). Paul said, "By the one man's obedience the many will be made righteous" (Rom. 5:19). Scripture anticipates this amazing truth ahead of time in Shamgar by showing us that God can save through one man representing many others.

Where do we, as it were, find *ourselves* in this verse? First of all, we are not Shamgar. Yes, we can imitate his faith and say, "By faith I can face many foes," but that's not the thrust of the text nor by far its fullest meaning. *We* are sitting on the sidelines with Israel as our savior fights for us. As Christians, we can find real edification in this verse because our God did this, and our God did something like this, but much greater, for us. He sent his own Champion onto the field to fight in our place. Now *that* is edifying. I submit to you that it is also the fullest Spirit-intended meaning of these ancient words.

You deserve to face every single one of your sins. They stand hostile to you, arrayed in impenetrable armor. Your sins are fiercer than the wildest warrior, each one of them threatening to bury you under the fires of hell forever. Can you face them? Can you strike them down? You would sooner subdue Leviathan! I'd rather face *anything* else than face one of my sins before a holy God. "If you, O LORD, should mark iniquity, O Lord, who could stand?" (Psa. 130:3).

If you break one of God's laws, you've broken them all (Jas. 2:10). Break another, and you've broken the entire law again, for you have attempted to assault the Lawgiver himself. Thus, each sin comes with the full force of God's curse. And you've committed sins beyond count, but their number is with God. Your sins press you like mobs, demanding that you face them. They have their own *message* to deliver: "The wages of sin is death" (Rom. 6:23).

Israel couldn't face these Philistines and win. They were too strong, but they were raised up against the people because of their sins. Their sin was the true foe behind every earthly enemy they faced. Every careless word of the unregenerate heart, every flare of hatred against an image bearer, every lustful thought, and every smallest grumble against God is enough to condemn us for an eternity of eternities to hell. That, my friend, is the sober truth. Aren't you *thrilled* that he sent Another onto this terrible field to fight in your place?

One preacher said he'd take a Leonard Ravenhill over 20 dead Calvinists; another said he'd take a Charles Spurgeon over 100 dead expositors. In the days of the judges, Israel said they would take a Shamgar over 600 soldiers. But the Christian outstrips them all and says, "I take Jesus Christ over *everything*." He is the One for the many.

HE USED A PECULIAR WEAPON

The Lord also saw fit to record the legendary weapon wielded by Shamgar. "He killed 600 Philistines with an oxgoad." An oxgoad is a shepherding stick, which is a few feet in length and has a sharp end for prodding cattle. It may have had an iron tip, but otherwise, it was nothing more than a glorified stick. The chief of King David's mighty men killed 800 with a spear; Shamgar had *a stick*, so we'll give old Josheb-basshebeth's spear the extra 200. Philistines had iron; Israel had common tools. But a stick in the hand of God is a majority in the day of war.

Goads are not unique to the story of Shamgar; we find associations throughout Scripture. Let's look briefly at the profile of this unassuming weapon. First, the words of the wise are like goads (Eccl. 12:11). They're like sharp sticks that are good for keeping people going in the right direction. You can't read very far in the Proverbs without feeling their prick. The eschatological Judge came uttering wise sayings; he lived and died and rose again to fulfill the Scriptures. He is their *point*. He used the goad of Scripture to work our salvation by fulfilling everything previously written.

Secondly, goads are associated with God's sovereignty. The patient Lord of glory noted this to Saul: "It is hard for you to kick against the goads" (Acts 26:14). His arms were too short to box with God. None can stay the Almighty One who "does all that he pleases" (Psa. 115:3). In this connection, we can say that Shamgar's victory was the sovereign work of God. There was no stopping God in Shamgar; who then can stop God in Christ? "As for me, I have set my King on Zion, my holy hill" (Psa. 2:6). God was with Shamgar, and it was his saving purpose to make him unstoppable. The Lord laughed at the Philistines and said, "As for me, I have set my warrior on my battlefield." The Philistines learned how *hard* it is to kick against the goad on that day. God was with the goad, and their every effort against it was futile.

How this fight looked exactly, we don't know. Was he moving like lightning from blow to blow? I imagine they shot arrows at him—did he grab them out of midair, or did God cause them all to miss as he danced between their flying shafts in battle? Did they land a few hits, only to find they had given him fresh fury in his vengeance? The text doesn't say. What we do know is that God was on that field with him, and no one could stop him. This was supremely true when God was with his Son Jesus Christ in his single-handed, end-of-the-ages battle for souls.

Thirdly, an oxgoad is a common tool. Shamgar probably just grabbed what he could find. His name seems to bear significance to this point as well: it means *sword*. Shamgar *was* a sword, if you like, and by God's power he could take anything in his hand and use it to purpose. When he walked into the fight, the Philistines no doubt laughed him to scorn. The Israelites probably laughed too! What they saw was a lone man with a stick in his hand, but really they were facing the living God with a fashioned sword.

Foolish though it is to bring a stick to a sword fight, the Lord was only getting warmed up here. And why? In order to show his wisdom and power in anticipation of the good things to come. Can you think of anything more foolish than all this? How about using a cross to save the world? A cross was the symbol of everything foolish, weak, shameful, and defeated. At least an oxgoad has a sharp point to turn on your enemies; a cross has points pointing *at you!* But God knows how to slay enemies with it. Jesus went into the thick of the battle with a cross for his own death, and with it decimated countless multitudes of sins and all of our spiritual enemies.

Shamgar was a legend, and I'm sure Israel gloried in the oxgoad in his day. (Did Aph and Chen[6] release a robe of it?) What then shall we say of the Son of Man's victory on the cross? Oh, that we might say with Paul, "Far be it from me to boast except in the cross of the Lord Jesus Christ, by which the world has been crucified to me, and I to the world" (Gal. 6:14). Don't you desire to see Christ and him crucified like *that?* The cross is the symbol of our redemption and the means by which we fallen children of Adam can yet attain glory.

This verse may seem dwarfed next to the titan narratives of Othniel, Ehud, and Deborah to follow, but in like manner does a tiny atom appear small before it is split. The gospel is like it. It can be articulated in a matter of seconds—"he was delivered up for our trespasses and raised for our justification" (Rom. 4:25)—but eternity itself

---

[6] Hebrew for wrath and grace.

isn't vast enough to fathom its depths. When Scripture says, "Christ died for our sins...and was raised" (1 Cor. 15:3-4) it might not appear to be saying a whole lot, but it is saying *plenty*.

CHAPTER 5
DEBORAH

Now Deborah, a prophetess, was judging Israel at that time.

Judges 4:4

We come now to an extended narrative. The old Puritans might have mined a thousand sermons out of it; we mortals shall take it at a glance. Our attention will be fixed upon the most prominent features of this portion of Scripture.

So far in Judges God has saved his people through a man, through an assassin, and through a single-handed hero; now he says, "I can save my people through a woman." Deborah was the judge at this time, but she's not the star of the show. Another heroine, Jael, is to take center stage—that fierce woman of legendary deed. Our text will be 5:24-27 where Deborah extols the Lord's work through this most blessed of women. It reads as follows:

Most blessed of women be Jael,
the wife of Heber the Kenite,
of tent-dwelling women most blessed.
He asked for water and she gave him milk;
she brought him curds in a noble's bowl.
She sent her hand to the tent peg
and her right hand to the workmen's mallet;
She struck Sisera;

she crushed his head;
she shattered and pierced his temple.
Between her feet
he sank, he fell, he lay still;
between her feet
he sank, he fell;
where he sank,
there he fell—dead.

Let's begin our study of Jael by blasting back to the Garden of Eden. Who was the first gospel-preaching writer of Scripture? It wasn't Paul. It wasn't Matthew or Luke or Peter, and it wasn't John. It was Moses—Moses the evangelist. The Pentateuch is *The Gospel According to Moses,* if you will. Subsequent Scripture makes it clear that Jesus of Nazareth is the Seed who came to destroy the devil's works in fulfillment of God's original gospel word: Genesis 3:15, the *protoevangelium.*

The *protoevangelium* is the regulating promise of Scripture. It is no exaggeration to say that Genesis 3 through Revelation 22 is the unfolding of this one promise. All of Scripture grows out of this verse as the oak tree grows from the acorn. It's the Regulus star in the constellation of oracles, the heart of the lion. This verse is king of Scripture and sits enthroned as the first and ancient utterance of the gospel of Jesus Christ.

What concerns us here is that in Genesis 3:15 the human instrument is the woman. The Seed *of the woman* was to crush the serpent's head, and we see this likeness in our text. Here God used an elect lady to save his people.

THIS BLESSED WOMAN

"Most *blessed* of women be Jael" (5:24). Blessed is not a generic term in Scripture for good things coming our way. Good things are certainly God's blessings, but normally when Scripture says "blessed" it speaks of *the* good thing, the good news of eternal salvation. *Blessed* is a redemptive word. When placed upon the backdrop of a cosmic curse, blessed means much more than a little temporary good coming our way. God utters this mighty word when he's up to curse-reversing glories.

She was "most blessed *of women*." Satan worked curses through the first woman. We were born in sin because of what happened in the Garden, and Eve was the instrument of the devil's scheme there. The Fall is laid squarely at Adam's feet as the undeceived, willfully sinning head (Rom. 5:12; 1 Tim. 2:14), but the first woman played her part as well. However, God in mercy intended to bring forth the curse-absorbing Second Adam through another woman. The backdrop of the Fall through Eve makes this blessed woman Jael a striking anticipation of things to come.

Notice also where Jael was when this happened. She was in her tent. You know what that means—it means she was feminism's nightmare, a housewife! She was keeping her home when all of a sudden wicked Sisera was given into her hand, and this meek and lowly *worker at home* knew how to, shall we say, take out the trash. "I was not the lion, but it fell to me to give the lion's roar," are the famous words attributed to Winston Churchill. Perhaps Jael was wont to say in after years, "I was not the dragon slayer, but it fell to me to slay the foul beast."

She was the wife of Heber the Kenite, of Moses' in-laws. Apparently, they had come to live in the land with the people. They attached themselves to the Hebrews and, in doing so, became identified with God's cause. Here they are, *Gentiles in Israel.* Jael reminds us of two other blessed women, both to be found in the opening genealogy of Matthew: Rahab the prostitute and Ruth the Moabitess (Matt. 1:5). God used Gentile women to help usher in the Savior of the world. Even as the genealogy of Christ was slowly unfolding in waking life, Jael the Gentile appeared, a foreshadow of this marvelous truth.

In summary, Deborah says Jael was the preeminent blessed one of all women. She was a source of blessing to others, and was in that way like Abram: "In you all the families of the earth shall be blessed" (Gen. 12:3).

SHE WAS BLESSED FOR HER BLESSED DEED

Notice verse 25: "He asked for water and she gave him milk; she brought him curds in a noble's bowl." The moment she laid eyes on him, she knew who he was and hatched plots accordingly. Milk is not a drink to slake the thirst of a parched man. Sisera said, "Please give me a little water to drink, for I am thirsty" (4:19). After a few gulps, he probably thought to himself, "Milk was a bad choice!" Clearly, Jael didn't give him what he asked for. The text says he was given curds. The old Authorized says, "She brought forth butter in a lordly dish." *Butter.* Perhaps she gave him these dairy delicacies because she wanted him to fall asleep—which is exactly what came to pass.

Her plan was not her own, it was God's. It says, "On that day God subdued Jabin the king of Canaan" (4:23). God himself was the great doer in all of this. We also see this in verse 20: "From heaven the stars fought, from their courses they fought against Sisera." Was there some sort of heavenly phenomenon? Did God cause Sisera to see the sun falsely and misjudge his direction, leading him straight to Heber's tent? I can't say, but what I can tell you is that God had Sisera *on lock.* He was destined to destruction, and the very stars of heaven were plotting against him.

This plan was patterned after the *protoevangelium:* "She crushed his head" (5:26). Behold the defeated foe, lying dead at the feet of the blessed woman with his skull shattered. As old Knox rendered it, "The Seed of the woman shal tread downe thy head."[7] A violent thing was Jael's work! Picture Sisera's bloody corpse pinned to the ground with the tent peg through his head. She used a hammer, it says: "the workman's mallet" (5:26). Swing by swing her wrath fell upon Sisera, to his doom.

---

[7] John Knox, *The Works of John Knox* (Edinburgh: Banner of Truth Trust, 2014), 3:444.

LET'S PUT IT ALL TOGETHER

May the Holy Spirit bless our efforts at capturing a few rays of Scripture's dazzling light on this head. At this juncture in history God the Savior saved his people through a woman, just as our salvation was wrought through a woman in the fullness of time. In Mary, another Eve rose up to bless fallen humanity. It wasn't angelic armies or peace treaties that cheered the hopes of Israel, it was a child to come. What hopes are often wrapped up in a child, in what they might become? And who, under God, brought forth this promised child? One who was "blessed among women" (Luke 1:42). Jael is like her.[8]

When God sent forth his Son into the world, he used the stars again. The heavens fought against the evil one when the God-man was born. Eastern Magi saw something so remarkable in the night sky that they saddled their camels and rode hundreds of miles to worship a baby. While the angels sang to the shepherds, God's stars danced in step with the gospel at the appearance of Christ.

Our Redeemer was born of woman, just like us. He partook of our nature and likeness, "made like his brothers in every respect" (Heb. 2:17). *Through the woman* means that God intended from the beginning to save us through a human champion. Jael crushed Sisera's head; Mary brought forth the skull crushing Seed of the woman. The infant in

---

[8] "Jael received the blessing, answering typically to that bestowed on the Virgin mother of the Blessed Jesus." Andrew R. Fausset, *A Critical and Expository Commentary on the Book of Judges* (Edinburgh: Banner of Truth Trust, 1999), 99.

the manger was the Infinite One come to bind the ancient serpent and take his place as the Last Adam, Lord of God's world. The child was fully God and fully man: "And Jesus increased in wisdom and in stature, and in favor with God and man" (Luke 2:52).

The people of Israel were oppressed because of their sin. Their suffering was the just punishment for their rebellion against the Lord, and in great mercy he raised up a daughter of Eve to save them. When the eschatological Seed appeared, he came to take *sin itself* out of the way. God killed sin when he spiked the serpent's head to the tree. By putting away sin, he removed sin's curse.

When the Lord worked eternal salvation, it wasn't any prettier than the scene before us; it was in fact far more gruesome. It is not without reason that Jael used a spike, for on Golgotha we meet again with deadly, skull crushing spikes. "He was pierced for our transgressions" (Isa. 53:5). Blessed spikes! Blessed wounds! Jesus bears them still. The ransomed of the Lord will peer into them in glory, drawing out the marvelous depths of his love displayed within.

In Deborah's final blow she says, "May all your enemies perish, O LORD! But your friends be like the sun as he rises in his might" (5:31). All of humanity is divided into two groups: those who perish with the one who has a tent peg in his head, and those who shine like the sun with the man who was pegged to the cross in their place. To which do you belong? Like Jael, Jesus now stands at the door and says to all who will hear, "Come, see your sin that

seeks you!" Come now to him, and you will be forever
blessed

CHAPTER 6
JAEL'S SCANDAL

She struck Sisera; she crushed his head.

Judges 5:26

The Bible records the sins of its heroes. It shows us their grime as well as their glory, and this fact lends to the veracity of Scripture. The Bible presents us with *real* people, and everyone from Abraham to Moses to David has glaring flaws which remind us that the Bible is not really about them. It's not even about imitating where they got it right. How are you going to imitate Jael here? By drugging your neighbor and using him for lawn dart practice? Or take Samson. If we are supposed to imitate him, the best we can come up with is this: don't cut your hair and don't drink. Well, that is perhaps enough to divide hipsters and teetotalers—and I say, cut the baby in half!—but the kingdom of God is not a matter of shaving and drinking.

The saints of the Bible are not set before us primarily as moral examples; they have been given to us as *examples of faith*. They were sinners just like us, and "subject to like passions as we are" (Jas. 5:17, KJV). Everything in the Bible is written to move us away from ourselves and away from men, to the God-Man Jesus Christ. We have before us the ancient testimony to the Savior of the world.

JAEL'S SCANDAL

This account of Jael produces a lot of question marks. If God working in this way sits well with you, you've either already worked this thing through or you haven't come to terms with what she did. The Hebrew midwives lied to Pharaoh, and God turned right around and honored them (Exod. 1:20). Rahab lied about the spies, and yet God honored her as well (Heb. 11:31). Samson's misdeeds, as we will see, outweigh them all. And yet, even he gets a Hebrews 11 commendation for his faith. Jael's deed is perhaps more questionable than them all. She deceived Sisera and then...well, no need to hammer the thought into your head.

Looking at the questionable deeds, we're going to see how God answers the question marks they produce. After all, he's the one who put the question marks there in the first place. We will see that even the question marks of Scripture are made into shepherds' crooks, redirecting the lambs to the Good Shepherd.

God's salvation through Jael looks suspect. It's a scandal! Just what is a scandal? By definition, it's "a perceived wrong or immorality that causes outrage." Biblically, a scandal is a *stumbling block,* something that makes people *trip.* Scandals cause outrage, and that's what we have here.

We can conclude a few things from the Scriptural evidence. First, Deborah the prophetess is so far from condemning Jael for her deed that she *extols* her for it instead. As easy as it might seem to say this was a wicked act, we can't say that biblically. Scripture justifies it; who can condemn? Who shall bring a charge against Jael? She won the commendation of Scripture, and how does one do that? As it is written, "by [faith] the people of old received their commendation" (Heb. 11:2). That fierce and blessed woman was a believer. What she did produces questions, but we must fix it in our minds that Scripture vindicates her.

Perhaps we see a historical example of this kind of faith in a Wicliffite English nobleman by the name of Sir John Oldcastle. He offered King Henry a written confession of faith. Henry refused it rudely, to which Oldcastle said, "I offer in defence of my faith to fight for life or death with any man living, Christian or pagan, always excepting your majesty."[9] That's right, single combat to prove that Jesus is the Christ. He had apparently caught wind of Ehud's war cry, "Preach the gospel at all times, if necessary use swords." In his defense, the chronicler kindly (and truthfully) says, "The differences which we now settle by pamphlets were then very commonly settled by the sword."[10] We can't condemn him outright because it was an act of sincere faith. I think Sir Oldcastle received the mantle of our friend Jael.

But we further distinguish. Not only was Jael personally commended, so was the act itself. "There they

---

[9] J.H. Merle d'Aubigne, *The Reformation in England* (Edinburgh: Banner of Truth Trust, 1985), 1:104.
[10] Ibid.

repeat the righteous triumphs of the LORD, the righteous triumphs of his villagers in Israel" (5:11). The words of the song itself are a "repeating the righteous triumphs of the LORD." Deborah was singing about *God's* righteous act. She ends her song by celebrating Jael's blessed and terrible deed because it was *right*.

We will never see God's glory here until we get our universe right side up. Sisera deserved his end. He was a fierce leader of a ruthless army and a persecutor of God's people. We should glorify God that Jael nailed his head to the ground. The living God rescued his people through this gruesome act. Blessed spike! When we gaze upon God's pristine holiness, we begin to see things clearly. Jael's deed shocks those who are steeped in humanism, but it rings true in the spiritual mind that sees God's justice in it. Not until we see the holiness of the good God and our unjust wickedness against him will we also see the exquisite rightness of it all.

There's an even deeper scandal here, a cosmic question mark: How could the Lord simply forgive Israel and send Jael to save them when they called upon him? These people worshiped idols for years! They spat in God's face; even under oppression, they persisted in serving imaginary gods. "They did not repent of the works of their hands nor give up worshiping demons and idols of gold and silver and bronze and stone and wood, which cannot see or hear or walk" (Rev. 9:20). And yet, as soon as they asked God for help, he granted it to them on the spot. Now *that*, my friend, is scandalous.

Allow me to expound upon this. How can God do it? This is a deep and troubling question. If Sisera deserved death, what about these idolaters? If anything, they are worse! The only thing that sets them apart from Sisera is that they begged for mercy. Is forgiveness, then, simply there for the asking? The Bible's astonishing answer is, *Yes*. Remember, this is *God's* scandal. In fact, *stumbling block* is one of Christ's titles (Rom. 9:33; 1 Cor. 1:23). He is a stumbling block because he makes sin disappear. The gospel of Jesus Christ is an outrage.

For millennia, it looked like God was lying. He was calling ungodly people righteous! David cheated, lied, murdered, and stole. Eventually the Lord in mercy sent Nathan to expose him, and in response, David confessed. "I have sinned against the LORD" (2 Sam. 12:13). And God *immediately* forgave him: "The LORD also has put away your sin." He faced earthly repercussions to be sure, but the Lamb's Book of Life would hear nothing of stain or spot in David's ledger before God. It was all gone!

Old Testament history is full of many such penitent Davids, and God forgave them all. Is he unjust? The devil saw him who cannot look upon sin become a Friend of sinners, and he accused them before God. Surely, he accused God himself of wrongdoing. "How can you call them righteous? They deserve your wrath and fury, not your friendship."

Now, God is under no obligation to explain himself. But, he has decided to give us wondrous explanations of what he's doing. He has righted the perceived wrong of calling wicked people righteous and treating them as such with a violent act more gruesome than Jael's. The tent peg of the blessed Kenite woman kneels before the Roman spikes of Golgotha.

God cleared his righteousness through this bloody spectacle, and with it, he answered every question mark. He proved himself both just and the justifier of the ungodly who trust in Jesus. He nailed his own Son to the tree and poured upon him the just wrath that we deserve. If the spikes were driven into him, then they will not so much as touch a single one of his lambs. In fact, God's justifying work on the cross is so complete that his justice now calls out for our salvation. Because Another has satisfied all the claims of divine justice in our place, it is not only not wrong, it's exquisitely *right* that he pardon us and call us friends.

When Jael did her scandalous deed, the people burst into song. At first, it's hard to imagine singing about a tent-pegged human skull; but, in the Spirit, they sang this deed as a triumph of the Lord. The eschatological triumph of God through the bloody cross is our theme song, beloved. In glory our hearts will burst with a good theme as we sing of Jesus and his love forever. Imagine your very own resurrected, glorified self, bursting at the seams with the triumphs of God's love. We have only the very slightest taste of such things presently.

There we will recount the wonders of the cross. "And the city has no need of sun or moon to shine on it, for the glory of God gives it light, and its lamp is the Lamb" (Rev.

21:24). The Lamb who was slain is the shining brightness of eternity, the *great light* to rule the coming eternal Day. Through his wounds will appear the brightest displays of the revelation of God *ever*. What amazing things will happen, we do not know for certain, but we do know that we will walk with the Lamb. There we will live and move and have our being in the fullness of pleasure at God's right hand.

Our closing question mark: Is Christ crucified glorious to you?

CHAPTER 7
GIDEON

The people with you are too many for me to give the Midianites into their hand.

Judges 7:2

The Bible literally means *the book*. It's God's book, and it not only comes from God but reveals God to us. And the revelation of God in the Bible is centered in his Son Jesus Christ. The invisible God passes before us in the person and work of Christ, who is the radiance of his glory.

One of the most basic rules of faithfully interpreting the Bible is that of context. Modern conservative evangelicalism pays much attention to this, for which we ought to be most grateful. Yet, not to be too *critical,* but it is possible to pay attention to the immediate context of a passage while at the same time ignoring the broader and ultimate context of the entirety of Scripture. The ultimate context of the Bible—that which spans the testaments—is God's saving activity in Christ.

The Rosetta Stone is the great interpreting key that helped scholars unlock the mysteries of Egyptian hieroglyphics. Well, Scripture sets forth its own Rosetta Stone; the heavenly Book interprets itself. Some scholars lean heavily on rabbinical sources in their interpretation of the Bible; some even believe we *need* these extra-biblical writings in order to truly understand it. Amazing! Behold, it's a new reformation, complete with its own new sola: *Sola Secondary Sourcia*. Nay, but we interpret Scripture by Scripture. The Bible is sufficient to interpret itself; and further, it alone can do so. The Rosetta Stone of Scripture is Jesus Christ, the stone of stumbling and the rock of offense. He illumines every passage and unlocks its deepest truth. It is our wisdom to keep the gospel before us whenever we open this Book.

Now, in context, what does the account of Gideon reveal about God? *That he loves to show his power through human weakness.* This is good news already! This is also the vein along which we will mine the glories set before us in Gideon. As for our ultimate context, let us keep in mind that God's power in weakness sang at its highest pitch when God the Son hung on a bloody cross.

GIDEON'S CALL

We begin with the sad and troubling truth that the people once again forsook the Lord for idols. Man is hardwired for worship, but he has traded the true Object of his worship for created things. One ancient culture apparently worshiped eels; a poet said to them, "You regard the eel as a mighty divinity. I consider it at best a delicious side dish."[11] Foolishness! Beloved, there but for the grace of God go you and I. Apart from his kindness in grace we would quickly latch onto everything but him who

---

[11] Quoted in John Owen, *Biblical Theology: The History of Theology from Adam to Christ* (Grand Rapids: Soli Deo Gloria Publications, 1994), 115.

alone is worthy of worship. Thus, the people once again sank into idolatry.

Salvation is God-centered. Thus, when God saves the people here, he means to put himself back on the throne of their hearts. False gods are swept away when redemption goes forth. The people groaned under their sufferings and cried out to the Lord, who sent them another deliverer, this time Gideon. Let's take a few swift glances at the son of Joash.

Notice first that the Son of God called him: "The angel of the LORD appeared to him" (6:11). Not an angel, *the* angel. I submit to you that this is God the Son pre-incarnate. I'll give a fuller treatment of this in chapter 10 of the present work, but allow me briefly to demonstrate what I mean by Scripture.

Gideon himself believed that the angel of the Lord was divine. "Then Gideon perceived that he was the angel of the LORD. And Gideon said, 'Alas, O Lord GOD! For now I have seen the angel of the LORD face to face.' But the LORD said to him, 'Peace be to you. Do not fear; you shall not die'" (6:22-23). Why did Gideon think he was going to die? Because he knew he had seen God face to face, like Jacob at Peniel (Gen. 32:30). The same awesome being appeared to Samson's parents, who had the very same reaction: they thought they were going to die because they had seen God (13:21-22).

This divine person appears throughout the Old Testament in what theologians call *Theophanies* (i.e. appearances of God) or, more technically, *Christophanies* (i.e., appearances of Christ). This very same angel, or messenger, is directly identified as the coming Son of God by the prophet Malachi: "And the Lord whom you seek will suddenly come to his temple; and the messenger of the covenant in whom you delight, behold, he is coming" (Mal. 3:1). Jesus appears of old not only by promise, type, and shadow, but also in his deity. As Jude has it, "Jesus, who saved a people out of the land of Egypt" (v. 5). The Son of God was active as God the Son in the Old Testament; it was he who called Gideon.

As for Gideon, the angel called him "a mighty man of valor" (6:12). But any temptation to view him as a military threat will vanish when we remember what he was doing when the Lord found him; he was hiding. Was Gideon a brave man? Sound exegesis has determined that to be a lie. Gideon was a timid and trembling soul when God called him. This is good news for us, because we are like Gideon.

What made Gideon mighty? Just this very thing: "The LORD is with you" (6:12). The Lord could say this in truth because he would be the one to bring it about. "Behold, my clan is the weakest in Manasseh, and I am the least in the father's house," pleads Gideon (6:15). "What of it?" says the Lord, "*I* will be with you." He called the weakest man from the weakest clan to show the great flex of his arm.

Gideon got a new name for all this, an inspired alias if you will. It came about in the following manner: That night he pulled down his father's idols, but instead of condemning him, his father defended him. "Joash said to all who stood against him, 'Will you contend for Baal? Or will you save him? Whoever contends for him shall be put to death by morning. If he is a god, let him contend for himself, because his altar has been broken down.' Therefore, on that day Gideon was called Jerubbaal, that is to say, 'Let Baal contend against him,' because he broke down his altar" (6:31-32). God was making weak Gideon into a *problem* for Baal. He became a divine taunt.

Like the judges who went before him, Gideon was empowered by the Spirit. But something is added in his case: "The Spirit of the LORD clothed Gideon, and he sounded the trumpet, and the Abiezrites were called out to follow him. And he sent messengers throughout all Manasseh, and they too were called out to follow him. And he sent messengers to Asher, Zebulun, and Naphtali, and they went up to meet them" (6:34-35). Already a great change has come upon him; all of a sudden, he's a herald, passing from trembling to trumpeter overnight. The Spirit clothed Gideon for declaration as well as for war, and he summoned the people in power. What we have here is Spirit-empowered declaration through a naturally timid man.

And yet, despite all the empowerment, Gideon continued to doubt his course, even up to the very edge of battle. How like us! We who believe are so many Gideons, filled with the Spirit yet limping along in doubt as we go. But God was patient with Gideon, and he's patient with us. "He knows our frame; he remembers that we are dust" (Psa. 103:14).

Now, how does Gideon's call direct us to Christ? So far we've seen the sufferings and subsequent glories of Christ in Judges, but the Lord mentions a third aspect in Luke 24 that hasn't been showcased yet. That aspect is of course "that repentance and forgiveness of sins should be proclaimed in his name to all nations" (Luke 24:47). According to Jesus, the Old Testament is also about the global spread of the gospel through the weakness of the church. In Gideon, called by God the Son and clothed with power from on high, we encounter a likeness of the apostles, who went "suddenly" from cowering disciples to powerful heralds (Acts 2:1-4).

This was an identity shift for them all. When Peter was called by the Son of God he also received a new name: "So you are Simon the son of John? You shall be called Cephas (which means Peter)" (John 1:42). That uneducated fisherman from Galilee became mighty Peter at Pentecost; Gideon is like him. It would even seem that Gideon's new name anticipates the name of the church herself, which is, by a turn of phrase, *Let the gates of hell contend against her* (Matt. 16:18). This leads us to our next observation.

GIDEON'S ARMY

After Gideon summoned the troops, the Lord said, "The people with you are too many for me to give Midianites into their hand, lest Israel boast over me, saying, 'My own hand has saved me'" (7:2). Remember that they were facing soldiers beyond count, "like locusts in number" (6:5). The Israelites don't think they have nearly enough people; the Lord thinks they have *too many*—too many to display his great power, that is. When the Lord strengthened Gideon, he was just getting warmed up. Here he whittled their entire army down to just 300.

This is relevant for us:

> Consider your calling, brothers: not many of you were wise according to worldly standards, not many were powerful, not many were of noble birth. But God chose what is foolish in the world to shame the wise; God chose what is weak in the world to shame the strong; God chose what is low and despised in the world, even things that are not, to bring to nothing things that are, so that no human being might boast in the presence of God (1 Cor. 1:26-29).

In other words, he ever chooses the 300 Gideons to overthrow the Midianite hordes of the world.

What it comes to is this, beloved: We are the real 300. Before Leonidas and Thermopylae, Gideon's 300 defied legions, which victory foreshadows the church in the world. We are the eschatological 300 through whom God wages spiritual war, taking up our weakness as his weapon. Against immeasurable odds, the church will ever stand victorious, because God loves to show his surpassing power in our extreme weakness. And this secures him all the glory as all God's people say, "Not to us, O LORD, not to us, but to your name give glory" (Psa. 115:1). So much for Gideon's army.

GIDEON'S WEAPONS

Just what weapons did they use to pull this off? Swords, shields, and arrows, right? No. "And he divided the 300 men into three companies and put trumpets into the hands of all of them and empty jars, with torches inside the jars" (7:16). *Trumpets, jars, and lights?* And yet the Midianites met their annihilation in the wake of these very peculiar weapons. 120,000 of them fell, and the rest fled. These weapons even seized and appropriated the Midianites' own swords and turned them against each other! Weak weapons like these were full of God's saving power.

To summarize, what we have here is weak leadership of a weak army with unbelievably weak weapons. Can you think of anything more foolish than an outmatched army using trumpets and jars and lights to fight an impossible battle? I can think of something that's more foolish than all of that: the church in the world.

Let's look for a moment at the wisdom of God in these weapons. The trumpets were rams' horns (called *shofars*) and the jars were clay. Do these strange weapons foreshadow God's eschatological weapons of warfare? They do. Just like Gideon was clothed with the Spirit to blow the trumpet, the apostles were clothed with power from on high to sound forth a trumpet mightier than Gideon's. And, like unto the 300, you and I have been given a trumpet, yet mightier than they held. What trumpet? The good news of Jesus Christ crucified for sin.

Some charismatics feel led to blow rams' horns at worship gatherings. Apparently, they believe it changes the spiritual atmosphere of the room. Well, if I blow a shofar from the pulpit next Lord's Day it will most certainly *change the atmosphere* of the room, but such clanging of symbols has no spiritual power. Yet, if you want to change the spiritual atmosphere of the room, so to speak, there is a trumpet for that: the gospel. Put forth articulate sounds about Jesus Christ and him crucified, and spirits will be slain. You will be sounding the mightiest trumpet in the universe, and God will own it with power.

If there is anything more terrifying than going into a battle, it's preaching the gospel to friends, neighbors, and coworkers. I say it in half jest, but I'm sure some of my readers would prefer a physical fight to doing evangelism. If ever we stood in need of spiritual empowerment, it's when we go to tell somebody about Jesus. The Spirit alone can strengthen our lips, and he is promised to us for this very purpose. "He will glorify me" (John 16:14). If the gospel is a trumpet, the Spirit loves to *bring the noise* for Christ.

Now, what about these jars of clay? When they blew the trumpet, they were to break the jars (lights were hidden inside until the jars were smashed). Is there any likeness to this in the Christian's spiritual warfare? There is: "We have this treasure in jars of clay, to show that the surpassing power belongs to God and not to us" (2 Cor. 4:7). The light of the gospel shines out through the brokenness of the church. We have bodies of clay that can be broken in his service, and as we are *cracked* in the cause of Christ, his light is unleashed through us.

The simple teaching of Scripture is that by speaking words and being broken in self-sacrifice, we can overthrow hellish armies. The preaching of the gospel at our own hazard is renowned in war and feared in hell: "And they have conquered [the ancient serpent] by the blood of the Lamb and by the word of their testimony, for they loved not their lives even unto death" (Rev. 12:11). The Spirit forges the blood (Christ's work) and our death (death to self) into the sole conquering weapon of the Kingdom of Light. With it, we tread on serpents and scorpions in gospel conversations. The Apostle John knew about the trumpet and the broken jar.

We wage war by heralding the Son of God and backing our words with our lives. Expect to be opposed, struck, and beaten down in the cause. Expect to be discouraged! Expect to hear lies, to be hated, slandered, and reproached on his account. Expect not to fit in. All this is to say, love not your lives unto death, or, as Gideon has it, *break the jar*.

Already some will say I've gone too far, but at the risk of further upsetting my critics (about which I have the greatest ease of conscience), there's one more thing I want you to see. The night before the battle, a terrified Midianite soldier dreamed that a loaf of bread came rolling down and turned the camp upside down (7:13). The early Christians also turned the world upside down with bread—the bread of life. Christ crucified is ever the living bread that comes rolling down from heaven and flips every generation of the world upside down.

Here's a closing encouragement. Like me, you're weak. I don't need to tell you that. But I do need to tell you that God desires to work through that weakness. He loves to show his *real* power through our *real* weakness. Every Christian can say with Paul, "Therefore I will boast all the more gladly of my weaknesses, so that the power of Christ may rest upon me. For the sake of Christ, then, I am content with weaknesses, insults, hardships, persecutions, and calamities. For when I am weak, then I am strong" (2 Cor. 12:9-10). And when you fail, the Lord gently says, "On your feet, little one. Let's try it again." This gentleness makes us great (Psa. 18:35).

Next time you're afraid to open your mouth and speak of Christ, remember Gideon. When he overheard the Midianite telling his dream to a friend, he was given a sneak peek into the terror that God had put into his enemies' hearts (7:14). The Midianites had a secret fear of Gideon, and in the same way, unbelievers have a secret persuasion of the truth they oppose. When you testify of these things their conscience within them sounds a fearful AMEN. So, take heart, and don't judge by appearance. Just *blow the trumpet* and *break the jar.*

CHAPTER 8
JOTHAM

But Jotham the youngest son of Jerubaal was left, for he hid himself.

Judges 9:5

In *The Hobbit*, poor Bilbo Baggins was frantic with worry when a pack of unsavory dwarves showed up at his door unexpectedly. Chief among his concerns was that he might run out of cakes. Naturally, the young hobbit was quite undone. But when mysterious dwarves produced their musical instruments, "the music began all at once, so sudden and sweet that Bilbo forgot everything else, and was swept away to dark lands under strange moons."[12]

Such is the ideal preaching hour. The living God opens up his word to us and, as it were, plays upon it that we might forget everything else. Ezekiel is a marvelous picture of the one who hears the word by faith: "[He] took me by a lock of my head, and the Spirit lifted me up between earth and heaven and brought me in the visions of God to Jerusalem" (Ezek. 8:3). My dear reader, may he carry you away to ancient, distant lands, and to a Jerusalem greater than Ezekiel's, as we open this portion of Scripture.

---

12 J.R.R. Tolkien, *The Hobbit* (Boston: Houghton Mifflin Company, 1988), 20-21.

The Bible is a story full of little stories that all tell the Great Story of the Hero and his Bride, and God himself is the master storyteller. Stories captivate us as few things do. Our little ones gather around storybooks, and movie theaters are packed every weekend with people who want to hear a good tale. Our own lives are even little stories of their own. And together as a part of human history and as a part of God's people we play a role, however small, in the Great Story, which God penned in eternity past. It is even now passing before us in live action. The story of Judges Chapter 9 will help us see our own place in the Great Story.

THE STORY

Gideon died, and one of his sons rose up and wanted to rule. This isn't an account of a judge of Israel, but rather a false judge: Abimelech the usurper. He exalted himself against the Lord and the Lord has seen fit to record it for our instruction.

Abimelech was the son of Gideon's concubine. He turned to his mother's relatives and said, "Which is better for you, that all seventy of the sons of Jerubabaal rule over you, or that one rule over you? Remember also that I am your bone and your flesh" (9:2). The people agreed and gave Abimelech 70 pieces of silver from their god's temple. Abimelech took the money and used it to gather a crew: "[he] hired worthless and reckless fellows, who followed him" (9:4). He had one agenda, to rule over Israel; but first, he needed to get rid of his pesky brothers. So, he had his gang murder Gideon's sons. Thus the men of Shechem anointed Abimelech as king with the blood of his half-brothers.

But, alas for Abimelech, there is no thwarting the Lord. He kept for himself one of Gideon's sons, Jotham, who was hidden and escaped their hands. When Jotham heard what had happened, he repaired to the best pulpit that he could find, Mount Gerizim, a couple of miles from Shechem. Apparently, Jotham was the loudest open-air preacher of all time.

He opened his mouth and prophesied, calling them out for what they had done: "Listen to me," he says, "that God may listen to you" (9:7). *That* is a prophet. A prophet does more than disclose concepts; he makes application to his hearers where it counts, summoning them back to the living God. "If anyone turns away his ear from hearing the law, even his prayer is an abomination" (Prov. 28:9). Jotham says as much from his mountaintop pulpit.

Mount Gerizim has served as a pulpit before; it was the mount of blessing (Deut. 11:29). From there the blessings of the law were pronounced upon all who would keep it and obey. Now, based on what the men of Shechem did, we would expect Jotham to make for Mount Ebal, the mount of curses for disobedience. Instead, he went to Gerizim of *the blessing*.

This shows us that Jotham was giving them a way of escape, space for repentance. If the Lord were bringing immediate curses on them, he would not have offered them a way out. But the young preacher stood there in

God's mercy. "The LORD, the God of their fathers, sent persistently to them by his messengers, because he had compassion on his people" (2 Chron. 36:15). Jotham stood up to bless the people by confronting them.

Jotham opened his mouth in parables. "To what shall I liken this generation? It's like trees that wanted a king." Now, this is all very in-*tree*-guing. He uses the parable to picture what had just happened. "The trees once went out to anoint a king over them" (9:8). In the story, Abimelech went *to the people,* but this tells us that the men of Shechem wanted a king. Earlier, "the men of Israel said to Gideon, 'Rule over us! You and your son and your grandson also, for you have saved us from the hand of Midian'" (8:22). Jotham unmasked their ungodly desires with his parable.

As he has it, the trees go to three different kinds of trees and ask them to rule. First, they go to the olive tree, but it says, "Shall I leave my abundance, by which gods and men are honored, and go hold sway over the trees?" (9:9). Similarly, the fig tree answers, "Shall I leave my sweetness and my good fruit and go hold sway over the trees?" (9:11). And thirdly the vine: "Shall I leave my wine that cheers God and men and go hold sway over the trees?" (9:13). The implied answer of these remarkably intelligent trees is an emphatic NO. When asked to be exalted, they say, "Never! You will not *bough* before us." They knew they were useful in their capacity and they did not wish to branch out into higher things.

But the parable goes on: "Then all the trees said to the bramble, 'You come and reign over us'" (9:14). Now, this isn't a blackberry bush; it's a thorn bush. In other words, it's fruitless. And this worthless tree *loved* their request. "Rule over you? Great! I've always wanted to be a king."

It seems these three trees represent Gideon, his son, and his grandson (8:22). Gideon was useful to God's people, and apparently, his son and grandson didn't fall far from the…tree. When the people tried to exalt them, they said, "The LORD will rule over you" (8:23). Apparently, they didn't seek great things for themselves. Often the most gifted and qualified men will not strive to exalt themselves to the offices they are qualified for, but those who are worthless and without qualification are too often self-seeking and self-assertive. They eat up every accolade they can get, just like Jotham's bramble.

A bramble produces nothing, not even shade. It would seem that this sort of plant was not to be found in Eden. The fig tree was there—Adam used its leaves to cover himself. The vine and olive were also there, part of God's original good creation (Psa. 104:15). But the bramble thorn bush is a product of the curse. "Thorns and thistles, it will bring forth for you" (Gen. 3:18) And yet the bramble is useful for something: it's very good at destroying other trees. Set it on fire and it will consume a forest of good things. Abimelech is like it.

Wilting was the close of Jotham's parable: "If you then have acted in good faith and integrity with Jerubbaal and with his house this day, then rejoice in Abimelech, and let him also rejoice in you. But if not, let fire come out from Abimelech and devour the leaders of Shechem" (9:19-20).

After Jotham preached, he fled. There was no post-sermon greeting line at the back of the foyer. The preacher vanished, but his word flew toward the mark. Unheeded, the rest of the chapter records how it came to pass (clearly, his bark was as big as his bite). The Lord brought this fearful fate upon Jotham's hardened hearers.

God himself sent an evil spirit between Abimelech and the men of Shechem (9:23). The wicked will ever be their own ruin. Other leaders appeared in the endless succession of wicked men trying to usurp each other. Abimelech destroyed the people; he burned 1,000 alive. Literal fire consumed them. Thus, the fools were rewarded for the false leader they chose.

As for Abimelech, he was utterly humiliated in his death. Another heroine appears to destroy him. "And a certain woman threw an upper millstone on Abimelech's head and crushed his skull" (9:53). He tried to cover it up, but God has bronzed it forever in Scripture that Abimelech died at the hands of a woman. He went down in infamy and dishonor. "What the wicked dreads will come upon him" (Prov. 10:24). "Thus God returned the evil of Abimelech, which he committed against his father in killing his seventy brothers. And God also made all the evil of the men of Shechem return on their heads, and upon them came the curse of Jotham the son of Jerubbaal" (9:56-57).

That's the story.

THE GREAT STORY

There are certainly moral takeaways from this story, such as, don't be an idiot, stay humble, listen to prophets, don't seek high things, and be satisfied where you are. But, is this all? Is there a reason that the Spirit inspired this passage beyond giving us moral examples of right and wrong? Yes. The Great Story is present here in shadow.

In Judges 9 we have a match made in hell: a usurper, and people who want to give him a job. They thus destroy all threats to the usurped crown. But, God kept a hidden son in his quiver, tucked away and prepared for this very hour. And the curse of his words manifested upon his foes.

In a truer way, there's a greater Jotham, the hidden Son kept by God in secret until what Paul calls *the right time*. Isaiah knew about him: "In the shadow of his hand he hid me; he made me a polished arrow; in his quiver he hid me away" (Isa. 49:2). God had a master arrow, a hidden Son, the mightiest of all weapons, forged in secret, to unleash upon the world. That secret Son is Jesus Christ, who was hidden in a deep promise and a dark shadow for long ages.

How do you think the men of Shechem felt when they heard Jotham preaching on the mountain? They had probably lost count when they killed his 69 brothers. Jotham took them entirely unawares. In the same way, Christ appeared as a sudden and swift arrow, taking Israel and the world by surprise. He mounted to the heights, made himself a pulpit, and, unleashing 9 *blesseds* in rapid fire, brought forth goodliness from the greater Gerizim

(Matt. 5:1-12). And his blessings were mixed with curses for those who would not listen (Luke 6:20-26). Jotham is like him.

Abimelech was not God's man. Christ is God's man, and he didn't exalt himself, but rather was appointed to his high office (Heb. 5:5). The trees in the parable were able, qualified, fruitful, and useful. Consider that the God-Man himself, perfect holiness and utter qualification, did not seek his high position and glory. "There is One who seeks it," he said (John 8:50). He was appointed by him who said, "You are my Son" (Heb. 5:5). How foolish for us to seek great things for ourselves! "Let us sit, one at your right hand and one at your left," we say, but we know not what we ask. Even our great Master was raised up by the hand of his Father.

Those who went before him were thieves and robbers. Filled with selfish ambition in ministry, they hungered for the praises of men and their possessions. They craved these things under a guise of holiness, but Jesus snatched their masks off, exposing their fruitless thorns.

Jesus is the eschatological parable sayer. He opened his mouth, speaking of himself as a ruler and whose citizens hated him, but they said, "We don't want this man to rule over us" (Luke 19:14). And a curse worse than Jotham's comes upon them: "As for these enemies of mine did not want me to reign over them, bring them here and slaughter them before me" (Luke 19:27).

The usurper was humiliated in the grimmest fashion. There he lies, killed by a woman who dropped a head crushing stone on him. Was it not the skull crushing Seed of the woman who said of himself, "The one who falls on this stone will be broken to pieces; and when it falls on anyone, it will crush him"? (Matt. 21:44). Jesus of Nazareth is the strong weapon dropped on the world, the mighty Rock that came through the woman to humiliate the wicked. The lowliest believer can say to sin, the devil, and even death itself, "You were slain by a woman," for it was a woman who brought forth the dread Champion and Savior of the world.

In *The Lord of the Rings,* the Witch-king of Angmar is the head of the nine riders. He was an ancient, wicked man who became a ringwraith in the Dark Lord's service, and a prophecy had been spoken about him in ancient times: "Far off yet is his doom, and not by the hand of man will he fall."[13] The wise ones of Middle Earth deliberated over this dark saying. They diligently searched and inquired who and when was being indicated in the utterance. All they knew was that a *man* would not kill him. "A dwarf maybe," says one. "Surely an elf," answers another. It was not altogether plain to the wise ones. But fierce Eowyn manifested for them all that the Black Rider was destined to be felled by a *woman.* The same was spoken from the beginning in our world, and Mary's Son brought the promise to light.

Let's end our chapter where Abimelech's story ends. "Upon them came the curse of Jotham son of Jerubbaal" (9:57). The blessing would have been theirs upon

---

[13] J.R.R. Tolkien, *The Return of the King* (New York: Ballantine Books, 2001), 363.

repentance; however, the curse struck because they didn't heed his words. Like unto this, God is now pressing everyone everywhere to a decision (Acts 17:30). You get the choice, the self-appointed or the real anointed. Reader, *choose this day.*

The greater than Jotham took our curse upon himself in order to put the blessing of God upon us. He was crowned with thorns, as it were, with the curse itself. The fate of the bramble became his. He quenched the fires of God's wrath to make us "oaks of righteousness, the planting of the LORD, that he may be glorified" (Isa. 61:3).

CHAPTER 9
JEPHTHAH

Then the Spirit of the LORD was upon Jephthah.

Judges 11:29

When it comes to superheroes and their powers, some have more than others, but no superhero has a monopoly on them all. There's always generally an equilibrium of power; Batman's brains ever balance Superman's brawn. But Scripture has all the superpowers. It can fly at supersonic speed. It has x-ray vision, discerning all thoughts and secret intentions of the heart. Disciples locked in dungeons have also found that the word of God can pass through walls. It is truly *extraterrestrial,* from another world. It has regenerative powers: lay your hand upon it, set fire to it, yet it will always endure. You can only hope to contain it; but then again, it can walk through walls. Scripture has all foresight, knowledge, and wisdom. And Paul adds to this list when he says the Scriptures are "able to make you wise for salvation through faith in Jesus Christ" (2 Tim. 3:15). Scripture has the super ability to bend whole persons radically to him. May the Helper, who came to glorify Christ, show us more of him who is the mightiest of all deliverers.

We come now to Jephthah. Grief fills his account. To read it is to leave a bad taste in your mouth. The victory was had, but a dread ending snatched all joy from his heart and left the people of Israel in tears. Jephthah was a strange mixture of worth and worthlessness, wisdom and folly, goodness and grievousness. And yet, Hebrews 11 sings its praises of him. Lord, help us discern our way on these troubled yet wonderful waters upon which we sail in Judges chapter 11.

JEPHTHAH

Cue the broken record. The people fell into idolatry, and this time, the Ammonites were called by God to chastise them. Judges 11 tells us of Jephthah, who was raised up to deliver them.

Jephthah was a mighty warrior, a *gibor,*[14] before his great calling. His half-brothers despised him because he was the son of a prostitute, and for this reason, he left. He had abilities to help the people, but they ran him out. He was one of those bright youths who are ill-treated by society and go on to put their skills to use in trouble-making. A gang of shady characters gathered around him and they went in and out, working woe (11:3).

The people, however, eventually called him back. They recognized his abilities, hoping that God might use this man to save them. We see his godliness in the manner of his response to them: "[he] spoke all his words before the

---

[14] Gibor is the Hebrew word for mighty warrior or hero.

LORD at Mizpah" (11:11). In piety, he spoke mindfully of the Lord's presence.

We also see his worth in how he reasoned with the Ammonites. Apparently, this brother paid attention in history class, because we find him making a specialized argument from Scripture to prove that the land was theirs. He recalled how the children of Israel requested to pass through, but Sihon refused. He met their offer of peace with gestures of war, so God overthrew him and gave his land to Israel. Thus, he concludes, "You do me wrong by making war on me" (11:27). He overwhelmed them with biblical history, and like Stephen laid his logic at the feet of his opponents.

His reasonings went unheeded, so he put down his word and picked up his sword. He resembles Abimelech, a half-brother chosen by the people, but in his case, the Lord did the calling. "Then the Spirit of the LORD was upon Jephthah" (11:29), most clearly indicating him as a judge. "Jephthah judged Israel 6 years" is the final verdict (12:7).

Yet, as he rode out to battle, Jephthah took things too far. Excitement carried him away to the land of Rashvow: "And Jephthah made a vow to the LORD and said, 'If you will give the Ammonites into my hand, then whatever comes out from the doors of my house to meet me when I return in peace from the Ammonites shall be the LORD's, and I will offer it up for a burnt offering'" (11:30-31). We know for certain that he didn't limit his vow to animals because when he saw his daughter come out of the house, he believed she fit the dreadful bill.

Even with this grace upon him he could, and did in fact, err. He went Howard Dean on them. Howard Dean's frightful scream cost him his presidential campaign; Jephthah's dreadful utterance cost him his only child and Israel's joy.

Did he have to make this vow? *No!* Vows are freely given. Solomon handled this weighty subject when he said, "It is better that you should not vow than that you should vow and not pay" (Eccl. 5:5). To Jephthah the scrupulous, we might apply the text like this: It is better not to vow than to make a vow that would break all bounds of grief.

What kind of vow was this? Vows, in general, are associated with free will and thanksgiving offerings, but Jephthah's vow was more specific: "I will offer it up for a burnt offering" (11:31). The first offering we find treated in Leviticus is the burnt offering, and there it says the burnt offering was made for atonement (Lev. 1:4). Hands were placed, sins were transferred, and the offering covered them. It was a propitiatory sacrifice; the smell of the burning animal was a pleasing aroma to the Lord to appease for sin.

I think this gives us a peek into Jephthah's heart: He's been living in sin, and yet overnight the Lord calls him and clothes him with the Holy Spirit to work deliverance. Perhaps his conscience was pricked, so he bargained with God: "If you give the Ammonites to me, then I'll give you the first thing that comes out of my house as a sin-atoning sacrifice." It seems that he was bartering for favor with the Lord. Swept away with excitement, and his conscience condemned, he looked for satisfaction from his own hands.

This was needless! God had empowered him to fight the Ammonites, and that was enough. Beloved, it is with great care that vows are to be made unto the Lord. It's madness to make a promise in the midst of excitement only to think it through later. Be careful what you promise to God! There's no sin in not vowing, but a rash vow will lead to sin and grief. As the confession has it, "by rash...oaths, the Lord is provoked."[15]

This incident should have ended on a happy note: "And he struck them from Aroer to the neighborhood of Minnith, twenty cities, and as far as Abel-keramim, with a great blow. So the Ammonites were subdued before the people of Israel" (11:33). If Jephthah hadn't reached out his hand to (as he thought) steady the ark of God's cause, it would have. Instead, the chapter ends with grief and misery.

"Then Jephthah came to his home at Mizpah. And behold, his daughter came out to meet him with tambourines and with dances. She was his only child; besides her he had neither son nor daughter" (11:34). She came out in gladness, Miriam-like to celebrate the victory (Exod. 15:20). Maybe he thought Mary's little lamb was going to come out first, but God determined that his daughter would break the threshold. Behold the chastisement laid upon Jephthah for his foolish words. He

---

[15] 1689 2LBC 23.3.

"returned in peace" sure enough, but only to be cast into the extreme depths of sorrow.

I think you and I would break such a vow—and rightly so! Jephthah is either very foolish or very pious, perhaps a dangerous mixture of the two. Zeal without knowledge has led to worse things than this (Rom. 10:1-4). He should have known this could only apply to animals because the Law of Moses expressly forbids child sacrifice (Duet. 18:10). It would seem that his detailed knowledge of Israel's history with the land was more a product of his culture than of deep Bible study after all. Maybe he didn't know child sacrifice was forbidden and was carried away by blind zeal; perhaps he was so scrupulous of conscience that he thought, "I must do this," flying even in the face of what he knew. The Lord knows. May he preserve us all from such recklessness.

What is so remarkable here is the character of his daughter. She's another Isaac. Consider her response: "My father, you have opened your mouth to the LORD; do to me according to what has gone out of your mouth, now that the LORD has avenged you on your enemies, on the Ammonites" (11:36). She gave herself with as much sweetness as she could muster, only asking for two months to grieve that she had no husband. She submitted in quiet godliness to the sacrifice of herself. It would appear that she was animated by great faith; I fully expect to see this godly young woman seated with Abraham, Isaac, and Jacob in the kingdom of heaven.

In one of the most horrible verses in Scripture, it says: "[Jephthah] did with her according to his vow that he had made" (11:39)—*Jephthah the fool.* He killed his own daughter and watched her burn. And every year the women of Israel went in remembrance of her to mourn her virginity (11:40). Jephthah never forgot that day; the taste of it was ever in his mouth and the piercing sight forever burned into his eyeballs. The chapter ends, not with the celebration of salvation, but with the remembrance of bitter grief year after year.

A GREATER THAN JEPHTHAH

Praise God that Jephthah is not our Savior! He didn't put our salvation into the hands of sinners who can err, nor did he entrust it to sinless angels. He sent his own Son to do it. "I have no one like him," he says, as it were, "who will be genuinely concerned for your welfare." Glory to God, there's a greater than Jephthah.

Now, why is the Old Testament so long and eventful? Why not send Christ immediately? Well, that's a question to dry up Solomon's fountain pen, but one reason is this: it takes an Old Testament full of types of Christ to give us some idea of his glory. Judges and kings and prophets must be raised up in a multitude, each one showcasing some unique aspect of the person and work of the coming one. All of them are summed up in the one man, Jesus of Nazareth. He fulfills all their glories and rights all their wrongs and shares none of their failures.

The Old Testament is not only for us; it was for Jesus. The Spirit of Christ, speaking through David, said, "in the scroll of the book is written of me" (Psa. 40:7). The man Jesus grew up reading the Old Testament and learning his destiny from its pages. "It is they," he knew by real experience, "that bear witness about me" (John 5:39). If anyone ever read the Old Testament rightly, it was Jesus. I wonder, did he see himself in the account of Jephthah?

There are aspects of Jephthah the savior that foreshadow Christ. Jephthah was a mighty warrior; Jesus Christ is *El gibor*—the mighty divine champion and dread hero (Isa. 9:6). He came to be born of a virgin and to slay the dragon, and he just ran out of umbilical cord. He is the Mighty One with the skill set to work salvation by himself (Isa. 59:16).

Jephthah was of illegitimate birth; Christ was *believed* to have been of illegitimate birth. "We were not born of sexual immorality. We have one Father—even God," said his enemies (John 8:41). He alone was truly born of God, but ironically, for this very reason he was perceived to be a bastard child. He was an outcast, like Jephthah.

"Worthless fellows collected around Jephthah" (11:3). When the true Savior came, he was also to gather worthless fellows around him, but he was to lead them into holiness and glory. We are the worthless fellows that Jesus makes into his disciples and friends.

Jephthah fought for the land possession that God had given his people. In the same way, Christ has won *the heavenly country* for us. He will dispossess the world from the wicked, renew it, and hand it over to his righteous remnant. "They shall inherit the earth" (Matt. 5:5). "The Ancient of Days came, and judgment was given for the saints of the Most High, and the time came when the saints possessed the kingdom" (Dan. 7:22). The Greater than Jephthah won this great possession for all who trust him; its time is coming.

God allowed Jephthah to make this vow, and to sacrifice his only child. But why? It would seem that God allowed Jephthah to brilliantly foreshadow the gospel in this most terrible experience. Jephthah made a vow and didn't know what he was doing, but the Almighty has sworn from all eternity that he would give his own Son as the burnt offering of the ages. "He gave him up for us all" (Rom. 8:32). Jephthah did this to his own daughter; God did this to his own Son. He vowed never to change his mind about it (Psa. 110:4).

Like Isaac before her, the willingness of Jephthah's daughter prefigures the eternal willingness of the Son to be sacrificed for us. No one forced him. He laid down his own life (John 10:18). The Father sent him to save us, but the Son freely gave himself out of love for us, with more sweetness than Jephthah's daughter. The Puritan John Flavel pictured this eternal bargain between the Father and the Son as follows:

Father. But, my son, if thou undertake for them, thou must reckon to pay the last mite, expect no abatements; if I spare them, I will not spare thee.

Son. Content, Father, let it be so; charge it all upon
me, I am able to discharge it.[16]

Jesus shows his love for us in Gethsemane. His hour
was upon him; the terrible cup sat frothing before him.
What will he do? He trembles and asks if there is no other
way. It isn't whips and spikes that cause the God-Man to
sweat blood, it's the wrath of his Father being prepared for
him, foaming in the cup of his fury. But the beloved Son
submits. "My Father, if this cannot pass unless I drink it,
your will be done" (Matt. 26:42). He hands himself over,
grabs the cup, and drains it.

Jephthah's account ends on a sad note for Israel, but
when the eschatological obedient Child appeared, there
would be no lasting grief for his people. "Do not weep for
me," is what he told the weeping women as he bore his
cross outside of Jerusalem (Luke 23:28). He told them to
weep for what would come upon them for rejecting him,
but for himself he bid all tears to cease. "Don't sing the
song of Jephthah's daughter for me. *I want to do this,* and
I'm coming back."

The death of the willing Son has become our song of
joy. Let's outdo the daughters of Israel who took four days
a year to sing the sorrows of Jephthah's daughter. Sing the
song of Christ's great love every day of the year. "Christ,
our Passover lamb, has been sacrificed. Let us therefore
celebrate the festival" (1 Cor. 5:7-8). Let this be ever on

---

[16] John Flavel, *The Works of John Flavel* (Edinburgh: Banner of Truth Trust, 1997), 1:61.

our lips: "the Son of God, who loved me and gave himself for me" (Gal. 2:20). May we sing this song until all tears cease and death is no more.

CHAPTER 10
THE ANGEL OF THE LORD

Then Manoah knew that he was the angel of the LORD.

Judges 13:21

L et us pass over the wonders of the Shibboleth (as fun as that would be to study) and go on to a man named Manoah and his barren wife. This unassuming couple was destined to conceive the mightiest judge Israel ever saw, save one.

A key word in this passage is *wonder* (13:18-19). The two disciples who walked with Jesus on the road to Emmaus experienced true wonder. Their hearts burned within them when Christ himself opened their eyes and showed them unexpected glories. In a moment, God turned their mourning into dancing and filled them with fiery awe. He did it for Manoah and his wife, and may he do likewise for you. Perhaps my great God will even use these pages to show you beautiful things for the first time, things you didn't know existed.

THE ANGEL OF THE LORD

The angel of the Lord came and prophesied Samson's birth to his barren mother. There are *angels* of the Lord, and there's *the angel* of the Lord. We will be studying the latter. Who is this mysterious being? Let's search Judges chapter 13 for clues.

Manoah's wife describes him in verse 6: "A man of God came to me." *Man of God* is another phrase we tend to throw around, but Scripture uses this title to describe prophets and ministers. Moses was "the man of God" (Psa. 90); Timothy was a "man of God" (1 Tim. 6:11). Mrs. Manoah recognized that the person before her was just this very thing, a messenger from the Lord. "I met God's man."

"His appearance was like the appearance of the angel of God." She had a hunch about the imposing person who stood before her. Could it be the angel of God? Moses wrote of him: "Pay careful attention to him and obey his voice; do not rebel against him, for he will not pardon your transgression, for my name is in him" (Exod. 23:21). Manoah's wife thought of this divinely-vested being when she met the stranger. There was such beauty, majesty, and weight about him that she connected the two: "He's like the divine messenger of God."

"Very awesome"—that is specifically what she noticed about his appearance. Another rendering is, *exceedingly terrible.* The word *awesome* signifies awe-inspiring wonder mixed with fear. This person was terribly beautiful. She didn't fear him so as to run away; she wanted to see him again. However, she was struck with reverence and deep awe at his presence—and for good reason, as we will see presently.

Have you ever seen something so beautiful that it made you afraid? Perhaps a piece of music has pierced your heart, sent chills down your spine, and even drawn tears from your eyes. Some created things are beyond our ability to fully grasp; they display God's glory in profound ways and put holy fear into our hearts. The heavens, the tornado, the booming thunderclap, these things are terrible and beautiful to us. What then must his presence be like who moves the skies, powers the tornado, and hurls the thunderbolt? It must be *very awesome* indeed.

"I did not ask him where he was from." Maybe she was scared to ask. In any case, she knew he wasn't from around *there*. "And he did not tell me his name." Where he was from and what he was called remain shrouded in mystery at this point.

Upon hearing his wife's description of the man of God, Manoah asked the Lord to send him again, and the Lord heard his prayer. The messenger appeared again and reiterated his instructions to them. Manoah then invited him to turn aside for refreshment and a meal.

His response seems rude: "I will not eat of your food" (13:16). But it wasn't rude; why then wouldn't he eat their food? Because he wasn't human, and he wished them to understand that it was no mere man who stood before them. He was a transcendent being.

Instead of giving him food to eat, Manoah offered a burnt offering and a grain offering at his request. And when the fire went up toward heaven, under the open sky of an otherwise ordinary day, this mighty Messenger ascended in the flame of the altar before their eyes and was gone.

His otherworldly departure put the angel's identity beyond dispute for Manoah and his wife, and their reaction should put his identity beyond dispute for us. They crowned the incident with worship: "They fell on their faces to the ground" (13:20). He did not appear to them again, and "Then Manoah knew that he was the angel of the LORD. And Manoah said to his wife, 'We shall surely die, for we have seen God'" (13:21-22). This humble Hebrew couple understood that the one they had just spoken with face to face was none other than God himself in human form. The ancient Scripture made their hair stand on end: "Man shall not see me and live" (Exod. 33:20).

So, who is he really? Moses gives us an answer, and Malachi offers another. But we have all the internal evidence we need from Judges 13 to say that the angel of the Lord is an appearance of God himself. But we further distinguish. He was distinct from the Lord and yet was himself God. He was a sent divine One. Yes, we had better remove our shoes because we're standing on holy ground. We are in the presence of God the Son pre-incarnate.

The Apostle says "No man has ever seen God" (John 1:18). *Ever.* And yet we read of saint after saint in the Old Testament who saw God: Moses, the elders of Israel, Gideon, Isaiah. Who did they see? They saw the Son, "the only God, who is in the bosom of the Father" (John 1:18). These wondrous appearances were foreshadows of the incarnation when the Lord of glory would pitch his tent among us; his coming to Manoah anticipates his coming to the manger.

This passage contains the golden key to unlock the door of wonder and see what they saw if we will but take it. What's the key? It glistens twice before us: "Manoah and his wife were watching...Manoah and his wife were watching" (13:19-20). Their watching brackets their worship.

What exactly were they watching? *The sacrifice.* Many hundreds of years later another sacrifice watcher was taken unawares and swept into heavenly wonder. Behold, a rugged Roman centurion stands watch over crosses outside Jerusalem. It's just another day on the job as three regular-looking men hang crucified before him. But as he watches he notices something unique about the One in the center. He remembers that this strange Man in the center was even praying for those who nailed him to the cross. As he looks on, sunk in thought, he notices again the sign hanging above this Stranger's head. It reads, "King of the Jews" in his mother tongue, as if written for him.

He's captivated. He's never seen anything like it. He's seen many crucifixions, but as he watches this one, his eyes are locked. As the mysterious Victim fades into death, strange words ring out from his mouth: "My God, my God, why have you forsaken me?" (Psa. 22:1). He rejects the sour wine offered to him and utters more peculiar things: "It is finished" (John 19:30) and "Father, into your hands I commit my spirit!" (Luke 23:46). Finally, at the moment of his death, the centurion watches him ascend into heaven with a loud cry as his body collapses lifeless on the tree.

At that very moment, an earthquake rumbles beneath the centurion's feet. Boulders are split and tombs are cracked open, and dead men of Israel rise. It was a typical day for him, *nothing new under the sun*, but all of a sudden, strange and wonderful things began to happen all around him. Under the weight of such wonder, words were pressed out of him: "Certainly this man was innocent! Truly this was the Son of God!" (Luke 23:47; Matt. 27:54). He was watching, and he tasted of great wonder. A mysterious Man of God ascended in the sacrifice and he no longer doubted his identity.

Friend, what about you? Are you keeping watch over him there? Are the eyes of your soul peeled toward Christ and him crucified? He is the heart and soul of the life of faith: "The life I live in the flesh I live by faith in the Son of God, who loved me and gave himself for me" (Gal. 2:20).

So how can you know if your eyes are above all else looking to Christ crucified? *You'll tend to see him everywhere.* You will find spiritual analogies all around you.

Some preachers are constantly taking metaphors from *The Lord of the Rings*. One said, "If I ever reference that movie again, feel free to kill me."[17] Well, I can't say that,

---

[17] Matt Chandler.

because I'd be dead. But why do they do it? They do it because they've read the books and watched the movies so much that it's *in* them. They don't go searching for metaphors; the metaphors present themselves out of the fullness of their hearts. *The Lord of the Rings* is ever before them.

If you read Scripture like that, the gospel will lodge itself in your heart and you'll be watching Jesus no matter where you are. You'll feast on him when you sit down to eat; you'll pursue him when you drive to work. Your heart will remind you, in your various activities, that there is a Better than food, a Sweeter than music, and a Greater than Batman (or Sherlock Holmes). You will live your life by faith in the Son of God who loved you and gave himself for you.

When it finally dawned on Manoah who this mysterious Man was, he was struck with fear: "We're going to die." Why did he say that? Because "No one can see God and live." What did he feel in God's presence? He very likely felt his sin. The more you see God's Man in the sacrifice, the more you will feel a profound sense of unworthiness roll over you, plunging you into the depths of conviction. Yet Manoah was not without a comforter.

His wife carried the day. And her words, echoing through time, still minister comfort to all who will listen to her kind voice: "If the LORD had meant to kill us, he would not have accepted a burnt offering and a grain offering at our hands, or shown us all these things, or now announced to us such things as these" (13:23). We shall finish this chapter by briefly meditating on her sweet consolation to Manoah.

She listed three reasons to expect mercy from God. The first is that *the Lord accepted the sacrifice*, and this is most assuredly true of Christ's sacrifice for us. The resurrection of Christ was God's *amen* to the cross. Glory to God, he accepted the sacrifice of Christ. It was well-pleasing to the Father. And if he accepted Christ's sacrifice in our place, he will spare us.

Second, *he showed us these things.* God did the revealing here. If he has fixed your eyes upon the glories of the cross, take heart, my friend. He "has shone in our hearts to give the light of the knowledge of the glory of God in the face of Jesus Christ" (2 Cor. 4:6). If he meant to destroy you, he would not have opened the eyes of your heart to such things.

And thirdly, *now announced to us such things as these.* The angel came bearing news of a coming savior son. "He shall begin to save..." (13:5). Many saviors and types were yet to appear on the stage of history before that blessed fullness of time when the angel Gabriel appeared to Mary. With what joy did he announce the coming of God the Son in the flesh! All heaven sang at the news. If this news has been announced to your heart, take courage; if you see the glory of God in the face of Jesus Christ in the gospel, take heart!

We who believe have a threefold assurance of grace in the wise spiritual logic of Manoah's wife. My dear reader, if you are not God's child by faith in Christ, the wrath of

God yet abides on you. You *do* have reason to fear. Eternal death is the sentence upon you for your countless cosmic crimes against the living God. Now, while there is yet time, he offers to make peace with you by looking to the sacrifice of Christ and trusting his mercy for you there. But I warn you, *come to terms quickly with your accuser!*

CHAPTER 11
SAMSON

With the jawbone of a donkey,
heaps upon heaps,
with the jawbone of a donkey
have I struck down a thousand men.

Judges 15:16

In our study of Jesus in Judges, I've attempted to take up what seems most clearly Christological. Two more chapters on Samson and we shall bid farewell to this wonderful book of Scripture. Samson is by far the most prominent of the judges. He's a rock star, the superhero of the bunch. And in chapter 15 he begins to rumble with God's enemies.

SAMSON

In our last chapter, we heard the prophecy of Samson's birth. Now, he's come. In Samson, we see God overruling and superintending his life, even his sin, to deliver Israel. In our first glimpse of him, we have a son of Abraham who wanted to marry a Philistine woman. Naturally, his parents weren't keen to the idea, but they didn't know that it was of the Lord, "for he was seeking an opportunity against the

Philistines" (14:4)—bad news for *them;* that's the wrong end of the proverbial goad to be on.

While enjoying his wedding feast, the people gave him thirty companions with which to celebrate, and he dazzled them with a riddle. However, his bride gave them the answer and he had to pay up for the lost bet (which he did most aggressively). He then left in a fit of rage, at which point his father-in-law gave his wife to one of his friends. After some time, Samson came back to reconcile with his wife, but her dad said, "I really thought that you utterly hated her, so I gave her to your companion" (15:2). This did not tickle his fancy, and he ransacked the Philistines' crops in retaliation. It was a hard hit, but he was about to throw mightier blows their way.

They took their anger out on his father-in-law and his daughter: "And the Philistines came up and burned her and her father with fire" (15:6). When Samson heard, he said, "If this is what you do, I swear I will be avenged on you, and after that I will quit" (15:7). Apparently, Samson was as diligent an oath-keeper as Jephthah, because immediately "he struck them hip and thigh with a great blow" (15:8). What does it mean that he struck them *hip and thigh?* It means he gave them the business. Stirred by the Spirit, Samson was beginning to wax warm against the Philistines. He began to gather a reputation as a live wire that no one could handle.

Naturally, the Philistines sought retaliation. They came with their army into Judah to raid it. "We want Samson," they said. So, "3000 men of Judah went down to the cleft of the rock of Etam" to get Samson (15:11). *Three thousand* went to apprehend this one man. This is Incredible Hulk level. If you intend to have a sit down with Bruce Banner, you had better bring heavy artillery and lots of men know how to use it. One does not simply apprehend Dr. Banner by oneself; the same goes for Samson. He's uncontainable.

The men of Judah went to reason with him. "Do you not know that the Philistines are rulers over us?" (15:11). Apparently, they didn't recognize their deliverer, and apparently he didn't think much of what they thought of him. He said, "As they did to me, so have I done to them" (15:11). Here is the very plain reasoning of a courageous heart, of someone who isn't scared of the faces and fists of men. "Tit for tat," coolly says the hero.

"We have come down to bind you, that we may give you into the hands of the Philistines" (15:12). And remarkably, Samson submitted to them. Judging by his other encounters, he could have easily broken free and fought his way out, but he gave himself up willingly. The men of Judah sent him bound onto the field, gift-wrapped for their enemies on the hill Lehi.

When the Philistines saw him, they ran with shouts and unsheathed swords. But as the shouts were still in their mouths, lo! *Philistia, we have a problem.* What sort of problem? "The Spirit of the LORD rushed upon him" (15:14)—a distinct problem for God's enemies, as the other judges have written in letters larger than Paul's.

The ropes fell like melted flax from his wrists. This was *real* power, that which works easily, like a hot knife through butter. When the early disciples were filled with the Spirit they spoke the word of God with boldness (Acts 4:31), meaning, the word grew wings and flew from their lips with effortless joy. Samson had power at his fingertips by the Spirit.

Once free, he grabbed the first thing he saw, the jawbone of a donkey. With this strange weapon, he flew in the teeth of his foes. God's champion proceeded to take the Philistines to school with donkey dentals; they all earned a D.D.S. that day.

A donkey's jawbone isn't perhaps the ideal weapon for fighting an army by yourself, but in Spirit-trained hands it became an implement of power. About a foot and a half long, this bone can be wielded like a hammer or mace. The dead donkey became a *beast of burden* to the Philistines; being dead, it yet *wreaketh* havoc. Many a skull was fatally cracked that day, as Samson fought God's enemies down and dirty in hand-to-hand combat.

A thousand Philistines subsequently met their Maker: "With it he struck 1,000 men" (15:15). The number 1,000 is a sort of mythical figure, representing epic proportions. Scripture uses it that way: "With the Lord one day is as a thousand years, and a thousand years as one day" (2 Pet. 3:8). Samson had his own amazing day of a thousand, when as many men fell at his hands.

After killing them, he thought a little boasting was in order, so he took off his helmet and put on his poet's cap: "With the jawbone of a donkey heaps upon heaps, with the jawbone of the donkey I have struck down 1,000 men"

(15:16). This is a pun in Hebrew. He made sure to get in one last wisecrack, so as to *pun*-ish his enemies once more. The Hebrew words for "donkey" and "heaps" sound the same, so here is maybe a sense of Samson's wit (warning: I'm about to go King James on you): "With the jawbone of an ass, I have assassinated my assailants." [18] Asinine! That is perhaps the run of it.

We see more of Samson's personality than any of the other judges. He was larger than life. And like unto our friend Lemuel Haynes, "he had a disposition for amusing remark and keen retort."[19] Samson could take his enemies in war and in wit; he could handle words as well as swords, boasts as well as blades. In this big personality, God shows us a single-handed hero who liked to trash talk his enemies and preach his own victory. Thus far, we've seen God work through armies and single leaders, but in Samson, all God's saving power is concentrated into one remarkable *personality*, a champion of superstar caliber.

After the victory, he threw his weapon away. The fight took every last drop of life out of him. But he called upon the Lord, who split open the ground and made a new spring that remained thereafter. The weary warrior drinks, his spirit revives, and it would appear from the end of chapter 15 that only *then* did the people begin to recognize him as their appointed deliverer. And the ground on which the champion stood was aptly named after his strange victory: the Hill of the Jawbone (15:17).

---

[18] I owe this thought to Edmund Clowney.
[19] Timothy Mather Cooley, *Sketches of the Life and Character of the Rev. Lemuel Haynes* (New York: John S. Taylor, 1839), 61.

THE SON OF MAN

We turn now to see whether Samson pictures anything about the Lord Jesus Christ. Let's hear the story again: God sends a single-handed, Spirit-empowered hero to deliver his people, but his people don't recognize him as their savior. They bind him and hand him over to the Gentiles, to which he willingly submits. God then uses a dead body to kill his enemies, and the hill on which he defeats them is called, by a turn of phrase, *the Place of the Skull*. After he dominates them, he preaches his own victory, and everything is taken out of him. But his spirit returns and God revives him. And that very day, on that very hill, God opened up a new spring of living water that remains to this day. And then, his people finally recognize him as the savior he is.

I wonder, who are we talking about here? We are, of course, talking about Samson, but I trust you can see that when we talk about Samson, we are also talking about the Lord Jesus Christ. This ancient Hebrew hero has something to tell us about him. His wild deed of Herculean deliverance displays the eternal, cosmic, final deliverance of God through the mighty act of a greater than Samson.

There are a few things about Samson here that I'd like to press home for our edification in Christ. When he dispatched with the enemies of God's people, he didn't use a nice, polished weapon. There was no flashing sword in his hand, no singing bow on his arm, no glittering spear in the air. He took up something undignified and disgusting:

a *fresh* jawbone (15:15), possibly dripping with meat and blood. Samson became an inspired penman and practiced calligraphy on living Philistines. They became his *letter of recommendation*, read by all. He wrote in a wild hand style with a gruesome implement.

Likewise, when the promised Seed waged his eschatological war, he used a gruesome, ugly cross. The implement of his warfare was rugged, refined in ruthlessness, but not in appearance. It also had fresh blood and meat on it. He battered down sin, Satan, and death; he struck them hip and thigh with the cross.

Around Samson lay piles of slain Philistines, "heaps upon heaps." On Golgotha Jesus made heaps upon heaps of slain sins. Moment by moment he bore their punishment. They were systematically dealt with as he quenched the wrath of God in our place. Our Champion left our sin in massive piles of ruin.

Samson's next characteristic is the most unique, and my personal favorite: he could trash talk. It's hard to overestimate the power of speech in competition. One of the things that made Michael Jordan[20] such a tremendous basketball player was his mastery in the high art of trash talk. He talked before, during, and after the game. He got inside players' heads and even ruined careers with his words. In his career-high 69 point performance vs. Craig Ehlo, at one point Mike told him exactly what he was going to do, step by step. And sure enough, even though Ehlo knew exactly what was coming, Mike hit the shot right in

---

[20] You know, the crying meme guy.

his face. Samson likewise psychologically overwhelmed his opponents.

The Lord Jesus Christ is like that. He loves to talk about what he's going to do, do it exactly like he said, and then tell you about it afterward: "The Son of Man will be…crucified and he will be raised on the third day" (Matt. 20:18-19). "These are my words that I spoke to you while I was still with you, that everything written about me…must be fulfilled" (Luke 24:44). "I am the living one. I died, and behold I am alive forevermore, and I have the keys of death and Hades" (Rev. 1:18).

The Lord taunted death ahead of time. Jesus told the Jews who requested a sign, "Destroy this temple, and in three days I will raise it up" (John 2:19). His enemies accused him again, and he says in the hearing of the devil, "I'm going to disarm you. Then I'm going to take away your armor. Then I'm going to bind you. And then I'm going to plunder your house" (Luke 11:22, paraphrase). Meek and lowly Jesus of Nazareth said, and did, exactly that.

Michael Jordan will serve us once more. Steve Smith testifies that one night he heard Mike say numbers after each bucket. "38," then, "36," and so on.[21] Well, Mike got his 40, bless his heart. Beloved, that's nothing compared to the Lord Jesus Christ. From all eternity, he's had a Book filled with names, and he says, "I'm going to get every one of them." He's getting his people, and no one can stop him.

---

[21] https://www.youtube.com/watch?v=7Ms02gNaYjk.

Soul by soul he brings in his elect, calling them by name and marking them off in the Book of Life.

What did he send his disciples to do? To talk! He empowered them to declare his finished work, and God's blessing ever attends that effort. His saving power is unleashed in speech, words, articulation—in the communication of ideas about Christ and his single-handed victory. The proclamation of his ancient triumph overwhelms sin and Satan even here and now. Oh, that God would clothe us with power to *talk ears off* about his glorious Son!

Let him talk to your enemies, beloved. "The man who, when he is attacked by the enemy, protects himself with the shield of faith," says Luther, "is like Perseus with the Gorgon's head. Whoever looked at it, fell dead. In like manner should we present the Son of God to the snares of the devil."[22] Present God's word to your sin: "You will have no dominion over me since I am not under law but under grace" (Rom. 6:14).

Finally, when God revived Samson, he made a new spring. He cracked the ground and brought forth living water on that very day and on that very hill. "It is at Lehi to this day" (15:19). It was created on the day of deliverance and remained into the authorial present as a living spring. The Israelites who heard this account could go themselves and drink of this very water.

---

[22] Quoted in J.H. Merle d'Aubigné, *History of the Reformation of the Sixteenth Century* (New York: American Tract Society, 1849), 2:241-42.

At the place of the skull, when Jesus Christ shattered sin and death, a greater living spring was opened. Even now sinners can draw from the wells of salvation with great joy. We are speaking of *present realities*. Hearing with faith, you are brought to that fountain. "Whoever drinks of the water that I will give him will never be thirsty again" (John 4:14). Go now, to the Champion who boasts, "With the cross I have crossed out the sin in God's crosshairs. With death I have put death to death."

CHAPTER 12
SAMSON'S RIDDLE

Out of the eater came something to eat,
Out of the strong came something sweet.

Judges 14:14

The sufferings of Christ and his subsequent glories are the burden of God's Book. On that very first Lord's Day, Jesus asked two bewildered disciples, "Was it not necessary that the Christ should suffer these things and enter into his glory?" (Luke 24:26). If sin was to be put away and everlasting righteousness brought in, if all God's promises were to find their *yes and amen,* it was most certainly necessary. The mysteries and riddles of Scripture must be solved, and Christ crucified is the answer to them all.

We will end our study of Judges with Samson's riddle. The word rendered *riddle* here shows up 17 times in the Old Testament, 8 of which appear in the account before us. The word signifies dark sayings and parables: "I will open my mouth in a parable; I will utter dark sayings from of old" (Psa. 78:2). Apart from supernatural revelation, the deep things of God are dark to the brightest luminaries; it is the prerogative of Scripture to unfold them to us. Is it then any surprise that the Word himself came as a parable sayer and fulfiller of riddles? "All these things Jesus said to the crowds in parables; indeed, he said nothing to them without a parable. This was to fulfill what was spoken by the prophet: 'I will open my mouth in parables; I will utter what has been hidden since the foundation of the world'" (Matt. 13:34-35).

While Jesus spoke riddles to the people, he explained everything privately to his disciples (Mark 4:34). The personal explanation of riddles is the inheritance of believers, and why should this not be the case with Samson's riddle as well? Shall we delve into its darkened depths?

A CHRISTOLOGICAL RIDDLE

Samson's riddle was patterned after real events. He quite literally tore a young lion with his bare hands and found real honey in the carcass, and shared it with his very real family. That is no analogy. Similarly, the gospel, the finest of God's riddles, is also based on true events. The cross was an actual transaction of real exchange, and belief in Christ plugs us into these real events, giving us very real salvation.

Samson's puzzle was *riddled* with unknowns. The Philistines would never have solved it because only Samson knew the answer. He was its only eyewitness, and he told no one what happened (14:9). This dark saying needed subsequent *revelation*. The same is true for God's great riddle in Christ.

Death is the great eater; it swallows up the fallen sons of Adam, summoning all with an irresistible call. Scripture also says death is strong: "Love is strong as death" (Cant. 8:6). What is stronger than death? Who can wrestle it into submission? God can. He used the roaring lion to give him and his family sweet food, an anticipation of the good things to come through death.

This riddle forecasted Samson's great deliverance. Out of a greater lion, death, came the sweetest consolation for Israel: "The dead whom he killed at his death were more than those whom he had killed during his life" (16:30). Samson took out more enemies of Israel when bricks and bodies crushed him than in all his life's deeds combined. Little did he know, as he propounded his riddle, that his own history was being spoken ahead of time; much less did he know that he was speaking in shadow form God's great coming deliverance.

Through Samson God has already said, "I don't need armies, I can deliver my people through one man," but here he says something further and more wonderful: "I can save my people through one man's *death*." We've looked at several texts in Judges that are candidates for that blessed Emmaus Road exposition; Judges 16:30 is chief. In fact, few texts in the entirety of the Old Testament are more to purpose than this one. For my part, I'm persuaded that Jesus touched on Samson's death, simply because of how well suited it was for the occasion.

We've traveled back through the ages to walk with the judges. Samson is the last, and he points forward to the greater dying Judge with an exclamation point. Is it not true that Jesus Christ destroyed more enemies of God's people in his death than in his life? By his death, he undid the kingdom of darkness and destroyed the ancient serpent.

Behold Samson in the Philistine temple. He is betrayed by his close companion, humiliated, mocked before Gentiles, and all in fulfillment of the carefree riddle he uttered that day. His enemies have him surrounded. The five lords of the Philistines offered Delilah 5,500 pieces of silver to betray Samson; the Lord Jesus Christ was betrayed by his close companion for much less. Judas said, "I'll do it for 30." The Lord calls it, "That magnificent price at which I was valued by them" (Zech. 11:13).

Samson became sport for the Gentiles as they crowned him with mockery. He passed from Philistine destroyer to the song of drunkards. Blind, weak, and shaven, God's champion was humiliated in the presence of his enemies. Jesus was also humiliated and mocked. Drunk with self-righteousness and power, the Jews and Gentiles paraded the Savior of the world before them in mockery. They gloried in his humiliation as he became the eschatological song of spiritual drunkards (Psa. 69:12).

All of the Philistines were present to celebrate Samson's defeat; the five lords and the crowds alike were there. Jesus called the cross the hour of darkness (Luke 22:53); all his enemies surrounded him as he hung there. His human enemies gathered to watch him die. "You who would destroy the temple, what now?" they said. All the powers of hell mocked him and threw their fieriest temptations at him in that dark hour. "Decimate these stupid creatures," they whispered. It is the decisive moment. There is God's champion, humiliated, mocked, and approaching death, and all his enemies are there, ready to be struck down unawares in the greatest checkmate the universe has ever seen. Death, the great eater, was once again to bring forth something sweet.

Samson's enemies died with him when they pressed him to death. His end was their end; in dying he *put away* the Philistines. Like unto this, all of our sins crowded to Christ on the cross as he bore their eternal weight. The eschatological Samson cried out, "Let me die with them!" He put away the whole society of our sins once and for all.

Samson was in broken fellowship with the Lord at his humiliation; God had left him because of his broken vow. Christ was also in broken fellowship with God. In great mystery, he who knew no sin bore our sins, and the Father turned against him. He was cut off from God! Samson didn't know that the Lord had left him, but Jesus knew it as he bore the sins of many: "My God, my God, why have you forsaken me?" (Psa. 22:1).

Jesus manhandled death. Samson manhandled the lion by the power of the Spirit; Jesus offered himself by the power of the Spirit as he endured the omnipotent weight of wrath. There was nothing left in that cup when he dropped it from his hand, and only then did he give up his life. John Flavel has him saying to the Father in eternity past, "Charge it all upon me, I am able to discharge it."[23] He alone was strong enough to take the blows of God's judgment and come out on the other side.

---

[23] Flavel, *Works*, 1:61.

All the saving benefits that come to believers come through his death. Samson scooped honey from the dead lion and brought it to his family; Jesus Christ tore death open and brings pleasant things out of it to us. He shares the spoils! The sweet stuff comes to us through the cross.

CHRIST CRUCIFIED, THE GREAT RIDDLE SOLVER

The cross solves all the riddles. Let's start with a chief among them: "Why do we exist?" Philosophers have queried themselves into the grave on this point. Simply put, we exist because the Son of God was nailed to a tree. God created the universe and everything in it in order to send his Son to display the highest revelation of who he is. That is why the universe exists and that is why the fall of man occurred, to show what God is like in his great mercy and love for sinners. The universe exists today because of Jesus of Nazareth.

The cross solves the greatest riddle of Scripture as well: If God is just, how can he forgive sinners? Higher than heaven and deeper than Sheol, man-made religions try to grapple with this mystery. Solomon has it, "He who justifies the wicked and he who condemns the righteous are both alike an abomination to the LORD" (Prov. 17:15). But how can it be? Scripture testifies plainly that God does just that: *justifies the wicked* (Rom. 4:5). Jesus Christ crucified for sinners is the answer to this riddle. God deals with our guilt by transferring it to Christ and forgives us through the cross (Rom. 3:25-26).

Another puzzling riddle is: Why do believers suffer? After all, aren't we forgiven? We suffer so that God may show his surpassing power in bringing good out of evil even in our own little lives. We are sojourners in this life, and when we gather in the heavenly city we will find ourselves saying, "Out of evil, he brought good. Out of my suffering, he brought me joy. Out of trial, he made me holy. And out of my death he brought me here, to glory!"

Because Jesus put away sin, even your very death will turn to sweetness. Its deep darkness has been transformed into the very gate of God's paradise for believers. The moment your eyes close upon this world, you will blast through the atmosphere to the Paradise of God. How's that for *something sweet?*

When Samson's companions found out the riddle, they said, "What is stronger than a lion? What is sweeter than honey?" (14:18). Clever. God answers his own riddle like this, "What is stronger than my wrath? What is sweeter than my grace?"